# OUTSTANDING OPERATIONS DIRECTORS

## 31 Case Studies
## Showcasing Excellence

**CHRIS EDGER**

**FOREWORD BY SIMON LONGBOTTOM**

First published in 2021 by Libri Publishing

ISBN 978-1-911450-76-4

Design and cover by Carnegie Publishing

Images by Helen Taylor


Libri Publishing
Brunel House
Volunteer Way
Faringdon
Oxfordshire
SN7 7YR

Tel: +44 (0)845 873 3837

www.libripublishing.co.uk

# FOREWORD

## SIMON LONGBOTTOM
*CEO, STONEGATE GROUP*

Operations Directors! What are my views on them and where should I start? The beginning feels like a good place and that was when I joined the licensed hospitality industry in the 1990s. What was it like? I joined a sector that was coming to terms with the Beer Orders and the break-up of the 'Big Six' vertically integrated pub behemoths. At that time, pub estates were largely unbranded, drinks-led entities, grouped around 'loose' market segmentations. Quite frankly, the Operation Directors (ODs) I first encountered were the senior policemen of the field pyramid: controllers and monitors, whose main job seemed to be hunting down rogue LHMs (as they were in those days) 'on the fiddle'! It was a male-dominated role, populated by bombastic types, with big personalities and loud voices.

Nonetheless, it was an exciting and exhilarating time as the industry was on the cusp of a revolution and I was in the right place at the right time! I was incredibly fortunate – at such a young age – to have started my career with Bass Taverns, where my first substantive role was that of a Deputy Manager in a Toby Restaurant and Hotel in Exeter. Having passed the test (getting up at 6 a.m. to open the hotel shift – working through to close down at 11.30 p.m.!), I was 'anointed' and given the opportunity to operate my own Toby Restaurant, obtaining a first-class experience running battleship food operations (a rarity in those times). This experience gave me an edge as I transitioned into the Area Manager role, continuing to work my way up through the ranks before leaving the corporate structure to join a small start-up business called Mill House Inns. It was here – in a dynamic and expanding environment – that I found my feet as an OD for the first time. A smaller, entrepreneurial environment – where I could take quick decisions – was an ideal grounding for bigger OD roles in the future.

So, when I re-joined Bass Taverns – five years later – as the OD of Ember Inns, I was ready! It was my dream job. I was catapulted into being responsible for investing millions of pounds in superb community pubs, many of which we had acquired during the breakup of the Allied Breweries estate in the late 1990s. In hindsight, I was fortunate to be operating during a period where harder formatting (to reach out to core customer demographics) and a greater sense of professionalisation was spreading throughout the industry. In order to be successful, my approach had to be so different from the ODs of the past. Why? The job now necessitated the understanding of greater FOH and BOH complexity, handling better-quality multi-site leaders with a more sophisticated leadership approach and fostering strong relations with central support functions.

As I write in my two case-study contributions in this book, ODs are critical in modern hospitality operations. In the latter part of my career, as Managing Director at Gala Coral, then Greene King and – now – CEO of Stonegate, I have understood the crucial importance of OD appointments; their *criticality* to the success of the business. Indeed, I see creating an elite cadre of high-performing ODs in my organisation as one of my most important tasks and I take an active role in all appointments, whether internal or external. Also, I make it my business to spend quality time mentoring and nurturing potential OD talent, fast-tracking the internal progression of the best into high-impact OD positions. One of the facilitators of which – I'm delighted to say – has been Chris's BCU postgraduate Multi-Unit Leadership Programmes, which have provided us with a rich seam of OD promotions.

When Chris first talked to me about this book, I understood what he was trying to do – attempting to fill a substantial gap in research and written material on the OD role! I am therefore genuinely honoured to be able to write this foreword, and support him on a venture that will be so welcome in the sector. In addition to his academic credentials, Chris has first-hand experience as a successful OD, and I had the privilege to see him in action early on in my career, when we both worked for Bass. I witnessed how Chris developed and coached his AMs, and it was no surprise to see him be so successful with his postgraduate Multi-Unit Leadership Programmes over the last eleven years, where he has trained and instructed so many AMs – many of whom have been promoted to ODs. Now – in this book – Chris has brought his OD research and empirical analysis to life, skilfully interpreting the accounts of nearly 30 senior industry figures (including some well-known CEOs, MDs and ODs). As such, I believe it provides a sound route map and toolkit for all those who aspire to be ODs, want to be better ODs or wish to develop outstanding ODs. Using the research he has captured, Chris has gone into great detail in outlining the core competences, practices and development mechanisms that support OD development and ultimate success. I only wish I'd had it to hand 20 years ago!

Of course, it would be remiss of me not to comment on the timing of this book. The COVID-19 pandemic has wreaked havoc on the hospitality industry. Who can say what the long-term effects will be, but I can already see it has caused my Stonegate team to become more agile, imaginative and collaborative. There is no doubt it will create consumer and operational challenges well into the future. But within the context of this book, what does it mean? Going forwards, under the shadow of this pandemic, the industry will need resilient ODs that manage and deliver change and take their teams along with them. They'll have to understand and exploit new operational paradigms, channels, service cycles and experiential requirements. As such, I am in no doubt that this book is being published at the perfect time – providing the perfect handbook and guide to aspirant and existing ODs wishing to sharpen up their practice to confront and conquer the challenges that lie before them.

I hope you enjoy reading the next 200-odd pages, as much as I did!

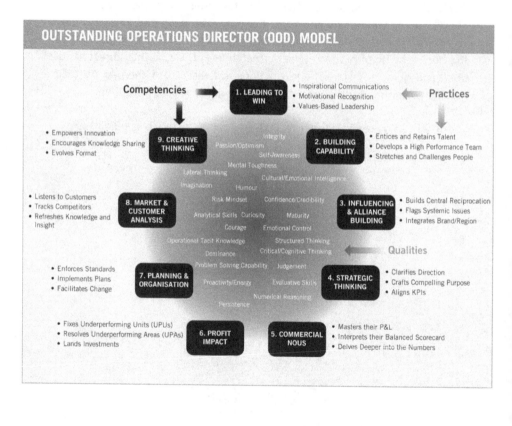

# OUTSTANDING OPERATIONS DIRECTOR (OOD) MODEL

Competencies → 1. LEADING TO WIN
- Inspirational Communications
- Motivational Recognition
- Values-Based Leadership
← Practices

- Empowers Innovation
- Encourages Knowledge Sharing
- Evolves Format

9. CREATIVE THINKING

2. BUILDING CAPABILITY
- Entices and Retains Talent
- Develops a High Performance Team
- Stretches and Challenges People

- Listens to Customers
- Tracks Competitors
- Refreshes Knowledge and Insight

8. MARKET & CUSTOMER ANALYSIS

3. INFLUENCING & ALLIANCE BUILDING
- Builds Central Reciprocation
- Flags Systemic Issues
- Integrates Brand/Region

← Qualities

- Enforces Standards
- Implements Plans
- Facilitates Change

7. PLANNING & ORGANISATION

4. STRATEGIC THINKING
- Clarifies Direction
- Crafts Compelling Purpose
- Aligns KPIs

- Fixes Underperforming Units (UPUs)
- Resolves Underperforming Areas (UPAs)
- Lands Investments

6. PROFIT IMPACT

5. COMMERCIAL NOUS
- Masters their P&L
- Interprets their Balanced Scorecard
- Delves Deeper into the Numbers

Integrity
Passion/Optimism
Self-Awareness
Mental Toughness
Lateral Thinking
Cultural/Emotional Intelligence
Imagination    Humour
Risk Mindset    Confidence/Credibility
Analytical Skills   Curiosity    Maturity
Courage    Emotional Control
Operational Tacit Knowledge    Structured Thinking
Dominance    Critical/Cognitive Thinking
Problem Solving Capability    Judgement
Proactivity/Energy    Evaluative Skills
Numerical Reasoning
Persistence

VI

# TABLE OF CONTENTS

# LIST OF FIGURES

# ABBREVIATIONS

AI – Artificial Intelligence
ALMR – Association of Licensed Multiple Retailers
AM – Area Manager
B-C-C – Business to Customer to Consumer
BCU – Birmingham City University
BDM – Business Development Manager
BOH – Back of House
CEO – Chief Executive Officer
COVID – Coronavirus Disease COVID-19
CVA – Company Voluntary Arrangement
DM – Deputy Manager
DNA – Deoxyribonucleic Acid
E&E – Events and Entertainment
EBITDA – Earnings before Interest, Taxation, Depreciation and Amortisation
EDLP – Every Day Low Price
EHO – Environmental Health Officer
EQ – Emotional Quotient (Intelligence)
EU – European Union
F&B – Food and Beverage
FOH – Front of House
GHRD – Group Human Resource Director
GM – General Manager
HMRC – Her Majesty's Revenue and Customs
HQ – Headquarters
HRD – Human Resources Director
IQ – Intellectual Quotient (Intelligence)
KM – Kitchen Manager
KPI – Key Performance Indicator
L&T – Leased and Tenanted
LFL – Like for Like
LHM – Licensed House Manager
LQ – Learning Quotient (Intelligence)
M&B – Mitchells and Butlers
MD – Managing Director
MSc – Master of Science
NHS – National Health Service

NLW – National Living Wage
NOD – Number of Drinks
NOM – Number of Meals
NPS – Net Promoter Score
NPV – Net Present Value
OD – Operations Director
OOD – Outstanding Operations Director
P&L – Profit and Loss
PCDG – Premium Country Dining Group
PPG – Premium Pub Group
REF – Research Excellence Framework
ROI – Return on Investment
ROM – Retail Operations Manager
SGC – Safer Gambling Compliance
TUPE – Transfer of Undertakings (Protection of Employment)
UPA – Underperforming Areas
UPAR – Underperforming Asset Register
UPU – Underperforming Units
VAT – Value Added Tax
VP – Vice President
WACC – Weighted Average Cost of Capital

# ABOUT THE AUTHOR

*Professor Chris Edger* PhD, MBA, MSc (econ), PGDip, BSc (hons), FCIPD, FHEA – Chris is an author, university academic and owner of the Multi-Unit Leader (MUL) Company. Founded in 2014, the MUL Company is a boutique leadership development practice which delivers one-to-one *High Performance Operations Director/Area Management Programmes* accelerating senior field operator resilience and progression in managed, leased/tenanted and franchised hospitality organisations (see *chrisedger.com* for further details). Earlier on in his career, after graduating from the LSE, Chris joined Bass Plc in the 1980s, holding Area Management and Operations Director (400+ units) roles before progressing to Executive Board level, leading Property, Commercial, Sales and HR functions in Bass Leisure Entertainments, Bass Brewers, Coors Brewers, and Mitchells and Butlers Plc, respectively. Then, having been appointed as a Visiting Professor in 2008, he became the Professor of Multi-Unit Leadership at Birmingham City University in 2010, whereupon he founded the eponymous MSc in Multi-Unit Leadership and Strategy (MULS). Over the next decade, his MSc MULS programme provided postgraduate multi-site leadership development to hundreds of Area Managers and Operations Directors from companies such as the Stonegate Group, Mitchells and Butlers, Greene King, Marston's, Premier Inn, Pizza Express, Le Bistrot Pierre, Oakman Inns, Mecca Bingo, Grosvenor Casinos and the Big Table Group. Completing the MSc programme had a dramatic effect on participant career prospects, with a 2021 UK REF research study establishing that 60% of delegates who had attended the programmes between 2010 and 2020 had been promoted into more senior field/functional roles following graduation. An author of thirteen books on Senior Field Leaders, Area Managers and solutions-based coaching (held in over 850 university libraries worldwide, as at May 2021), his case studies, models and analytics have been widely used on his postgraduate and Multi-Unit Leader Company programmes. He has presented the findings of his research at numerous Propel Masterclass events, also providing commentary in media outlets such as Propel Info, Retail Week, the *Guardian*, the *Daily Telegraph*, BBC Midlands Today and ITV Central. Holding a PhD from the Warwick Business School for his research into 'executive behaviour during critical events', he is starting a postgraduate history degree – in order to research 'early modern' tied trade pub evolution – at the University of Oxford in October 2021.

# ACKNOWLEDGEMENTS

The author would like to thank (in case-study order) the contributors to this book: Simon Longbottom (CEO, Stonegate Group), Gavin Smith (Managing Director, Pizza Pilgrims), Clive Chesser (CEO, Punch Pubs & Co), Adam Fowle (ex-Senior Non-Executive Director, Ei Group), Martin Nelson (Operations Director, Premium Country Pubs, Mitchells and Butlers), Helen Charlesworth (Executive Managing Director, Stonegate Group), Steve Worrall (Managing Director, St Austell Pubs, Inns & Hotels), Vanessa Hall (ex-Chair and CEO, Vapiano S.E.), David Singleton (ex-Regional Vice President, Hard Rock Cafe), Liz Phillips (ex-HRD Macdonald Hotels, Krispy Kreme, Swissport, Orchid Pubs, and Mitchells and Butlers), Mike O'Connor (Operations Director, Greene King Pub Partners), Keith Palmer (National Town Centre Operations Manager, Marston's), Karen Forrester (ex-CEO of TGI Fridays), Colin Hawkins (Divisional Operations Director, Stonegate Group), James Pavey (National Operations Director, Tesco Cafés), Adrian Frid (National Operations Director, Caffè Nero UK), Doug Wright DL, HonDoc (CEO of Wright Restaurants T/A McDonald's Restaurant), Susan Chappell (Executive Divisional MD, City Division, Mitchells and Butlers), Elton Gray (Commercial and Operations Director, Creams Café), John Dyson (National Operations Director, Mecca Bingo), Jon Walters (Operations Director, Qbic Hotels), Elaine Kennedy (Operations Director, Hawthorn (The Community Pub Company)), Barrie Robinson (National Operations Director, Parkdean Resorts), Alex Ford (Managing Director, Oakman Inns), Stephen Gould (Managing Director, Everards), Scott Fowler (Operations Director, Eastern Division, Whitbread Restaurants) and Ric Fyfe (Operations Director, Scotland and Northern Ireland, Gather & Gather).

*To Sheenagh*

# INTRODUCTION

Operations Directors (ODs) – the 'leaders of Area Managers' – are *pivotal* to multi-unit hospitality success! As senior field executives, they are the key *linkage and interface* between central strategy and local operations. Also, their capacity to provide *inspiring leadership, creating a winning, 'can do' regional/ brand culture* – particularly during adverse circumstances – is critical in an industry that exists to provide *atmosphere, warmth, sociability and conviviality*. ODs are the key drivers in *setting the climate* to ensure their Area Managers and wider regional/brand teams generate *uplifting, memorable and distinctive experiences* for their customers.

However, virtually nothing has been written about their role and – as a cohort – they remain woefully under-researched. This means that aspirant ODs – most commonly Area Managers – have virtually nothing (in published form) to read and reflect upon, or provide them with insights on what is one of the most *stressful, demanding and stretching assignments* within multi-unit hospitality due to the role's exposure to:

- **Distance**: ODs are further detached from front-line operations and guests than their AMs/BDMs and are called upon to exert an inordinate amount of effort to close down high degrees of psychological and geographical distance if they are to 'make their mark'. As such, the role requires high levels of contagious optimism, humour, energy and stamina which – if poorly 'paced' or 'over-indexed' – can cause burn out and failure.
- **Paradox**: in addition, ODs in this sector are confronted by the 'hospitality paradox', namely: that an industry that professes the necessity to deliver highly interactive, memorable service encounters, largely employs low-paid, youthful, transient front-line teams and foreign-national kitchen crews who perceive themselves as being exploited as 'sweat labour' and are only present due to 'low barriers to entry' and 'constrained career choices'!
- **Scale**: also, in large corporates, ODs are accountable for huge P&Ls, with wide spans of portfolio control – meaning they are placed under a great deal of pressure. Poor leadership and commercial missteps at this level can prove extremely costly and difficult to unpick. The risk to companies of making the wrong appointment at this level is huge.

1

- **Scarcity**: ODs typically have to achieve improbable commercial objectives with limited resources (i.e. capital, talent, functional support, etc.). The focus and energy required to build up regional/brand self-sufficiency to optimise performance – in amongst all the 'noise' – can prove demanding and draining.

- **Complexity**: in smaller hospitality companies or start-ups, ODs will have responsibilities stretching beyond operational line leadership, increasing the complexity of the role. In large corporates, ODs have to build relationships with multiple functional stakeholders to provide technical assistance and back-up. If the role purely involved field leadership, it would be relatively straightforward; its wider remit (including format/product development, portfolio investment, pricing strategy, landing new processes/initiatives, etc.) requires judgement, resilience and high levels of intellectual and emotional intelligence.

- **Disruption**: hospitality companies never stand still: they are either growing or contracting due to changes in consumer behaviour and/or competitive pressure! Also, the recent COVID pandemic has wrought apocalyptic changes upon the industry (see Chapter One) which – with its strains, variants and mutations – might reverberate for years. ODs are on the front-line of dealing and coping with this disruption – attempting to 'future proof' their operations for sustainable commercial viability – activities that require agility, resourcefulness and responsiveness.

It is because of these reasons – distance, paradox, scale, resource scarcity, complexity and disruption – that many operators transitioning into the OD role experience *outright failure* or *delayed performance*. Thus, a book highlighting how outstanding ODs overcome these challenges – increasing their 'stickability' and commercial impact – would be useful to aspirant ODs and their developers. This book – the outcome of an intensive research exercise – is my modest contribution to providing some empirical insight into the core dynamics of the role.

But how did I research this book? *First*, I was able to draw on the research of my eight hundred or so postgraduate Multi-Unit Leadership and Strategy students over the last decade (from companies such as Stonegate Group, Mitchells and Butlers, Marston's, Greene King, Oakman Inns, Pizza Express, Casual Dining Group, Premier Inn, Mecca Bingo, Grosvenor Casinos, etc.) – many of whom have since been promoted to OD level and beyond – to frame a number of research questions relating to outstanding OD practice.

*Second* – using these research questions as a base – I consulted a panel of five hospitality-industry 'notables' to sense check the *challenges, competencies* and *capability requirements* relating to the role. *Third*, this led me to frame a *structured questionnaire* (see Figure 1) which – from June 2020 to March 2021 (during the traumatic disruption of COVID) – provided the basis for me to interview and collect case studies from twenty-seven senior executives (CEOs, MDs and ODs) within the UK hospitality industry to shed light upon the following questions:

**'The Leader of Area Managers – How to Be an Outstanding Operations Director'**

**Senior Executive/Exec Director – Generic Questions**

**A. Select the top 3 most *significant differences* between the Area Manager/BDM and Operations Director roles from the following:**

1. Strategic Thinking (long-term rather than short-term)
2. Alliance Building (with Central Stakeholders)
3. Planning and Organisation (with longer time horizons)
4. Portfolio Investment (allocating capital across the Region/Brand)
5. Experiential and Product Innovation (conceiving differentiation and landing it)
6. Market and Customer Analysis (complex analytics)
7. Inspirational Leadership (at a greater psychological and geographical distance)
8. *Any Other* ....

**B. Select the top 3 methods of internally *identifying potential* Operations Directors from the following:**

1. Consistently high Area Management/BDM performance? (always upper quartile)
2. Appraisals? (hi-potential rating)
3. Assessment Centres? (verbal and cognitive reasoning?)
4. Fast-Track Talent Schemes? (structured development and education)
5. Coaching/Mentoring Programmes?
6. Deputy/Senior AM Performance? (impact deputising)
7. Exec Talent Management discussions? (other stakeholder views?)
8. Senior Sponsorship? (AM has a senior advocate that they have worked for before!)
9. *Any Other* .... (doing something famous?)

**C. Select the top 3 *development mechanisms* to prepare Area Managers for the Operations Director role from the following**

1. Interim OD roles? (covering for absence or secondments)
2. Strawberry-patch OD Roles? (i.e. Operations Manager with 3-4 Area Managers)
3. Working at the Centre in a Functional Role? (permanent or seconded)
4. Central Project Management roles? (seconded or voluntary)
5. Executive Education? (cognitive development)
6. Senior Mentoring/Coaching? (by a Senior Field Executive)
7. *Any other?*

**D. Select the top 3 required OD *role competencies* from the following:**

#1 = Commercial Nous

#2 = Strategic Thinking

#3 = Leading to Win

#4 = Building Capability

#5 = Planning and Organising

#6 = Profit Focus

#7 = Market and Customer Analysis

#8 = Creative Thinking

#9 = Influencing and Alliance Building

**E. Select the top 2 *technical competencies* that ODs will need to develop - to outperform their peers - over the next 10 years from the following:**

1. Project Management
2. Data Analysis
3. Digital Sales and Marketing
4. Artificial Intelligence and Service Mechanisation
5. Customer Experience Design
6. Well-being Counselling (professional proficiency)

**F. Subsidiary Questions**

WHAT - IN YOUR VIEW ARE THE MAIN CHARACTERISTICS OF POOR ODs?

What is the optimal OD/AM span of control? (how many AMs should report in to them?)

What is their optimal size of portfolio? (how many units should they have responsibility for?)

Why do so many companies opt to go externally for OD appointments?

Do 'lifer' AMs make better ODs than 'lifer' functional appointments?

Why are so few female AMs appointed to OD positions?

Do graduate ODs outperform non-graduate ODs?

What types of ODs do businesses usually lack? (entrepreneurs, scalers, evolvers or turnaround specialists?)

What are the different skills requirements for ODs that run:

- Unbranded formats (managed)
- Multi-Brand formats (managed)
- Single Brand formats (managed)
- Unbranded formats (leased/tenanted)
- Single Brand formats (franchised)

**Figure 1: Outstanding OD Research Questionnaire**

Quite simply, the findings and implications of the answers from the twenty-seven respondents to the questionnaire in Figure 1 above – allied to the thirty-one case studies they contributed – form the content of this book, giving us a better understanding of what constitutes outstanding OD practice, overcoming and ameliorating some of the aforementioned challenges of the role. If you wish to read more generic books on branded, franchised or emotional leadership, feel free to read previous books I have written in these areas[1]. This book will solely focus on interpreting the questionnaire data and case-study evidence I collected from the twenty-seven executive respondents to increase our understanding as to what outstanding ODs do in managed, leased/tenanted and franchised hospitality operations.

Accordingly, this book is divided into three distinct sections. The first section will analyse the context in which ODs operate and the *industrial, organisational and personal challenges* they face. The second section will examine the *role* and then outline (in rank order) the *nine competencies of outstanding ODs*, with supportive illustrative case studies showcasing *best practice*. The third section will unpack how best to *nurture and develop outstanding ODs*. The conclusion will bring all the sections together by advancing an *integrated OOD Model and Framework* that should assist all aspirant ODs and their developers. In all sections, my 'binding narrative' will be kept to a minimum as I use the thoughts and insights from this book's contributors as its dynamic voice.

But – building on my opening comments – *why* are Operations Directors so pivotal? The following contribution from Simon Longbottom will provide you with up-front insights (which will reverberate during the rest of the book) as to why the role is so important and what the best do.

---

1   The most useful texts being: Edger, C., and Heffernan, N., *Advanced Leader Coaching – Accelerating Personal, Interpersonal and Business Growth* (Oxford: Libri, 2020); Edger, C., and Hughes, T., *Inspirational Leadership – Mobilising Super-performance Through Emotion* (Oxford: Libri, 2017); and Edger, C., and Hughes, T., *Effective Brand Leadership – Be Different. Stay Different. Or Perish!* (Oxford: Libri, 2016).

## CASE STUDY 1 – WHAT DO OUTSTANDING OPERATIONS DIRECTORS DO!?

*Simon Longbottom has been the CEO of Stonegate since 2014, building it up to become the largest pub company in the UK by 2020. Previously the MD of Gala and Greene King, he was elected to the Maserati 100 list of the UK's top entrepreneurs and crowned Leader of the Year at the Publican Awards in 2019.*

The Operations Director role is one of the most important field roles within multi-site hospitality and leisure organisations. They are the articulators, integrators and synthesisers of the company's mission and intent, whilst – simultaneously – being the guardians and experts of their people, assets and local markets. It is their mastery of this fusion – articulating central strategy, whilst optimising local opportunity – that marks the best out from the rest. They also get that they are in the *memory* business! Hospitality is about creating *vibrant social spaces*, generating *great experiences* for customers so that they tell their friends and keep coming back time and again! But how do they do it? I would pick out seven key factors in their success:

- **Create Trench Spirit**: really good ODs are great at imbuing elite tribes with what I call 'trench spirit': when the going gets tough, they've got teamers who will go over the top with them to capture back competitive territory! Through their passion and determination – conveyed through a high level of visibility and sparkling oratory at their bi-annual regional conferences – they inculcate their people with a deep sense of purpose and mission. Of course, some ODs can take this too far; trying to declare UDI from the corporate centre or encouraging their followers to 'blow up' corporate bridges in pursuit of narrow regional aims! But the great OD is able to carefully manage these boundary tensions whilst creating a vibrant 'esprit de corps'.

- **Break Down Barriers**: in tandem with this, great ODs combine visibility with credibility within their region/brand. The two are interlinked – the former bolstering the latter. By being visibly 'in' the business at key trading sessions (nights and weekends), they break down barriers between themselves and their front-line teams. By doing this, they demonstrate that they are not 'part of

7

the machinery at HQ' – detached, distant and impersonal. They are close, on their side and with them! This enhances their credibility, showing that they are emotionally vested in the business. This is a useful emotional bank account for them to draw on when times get tough.

- **Resolve Big Bleeders**: outstanding ODs are also great at getting units that are bleeding sales, profit and cash working again – quickly. They have this ability to go into big problem sites, spend 30–45 minutes 'sensing' and diagnosing the situation. It's a deep tacit skill, crafted over years of field leadership. It's not formulaic as such (although they certainly know the data back-to-front); it's about analysing, processing and assessing the situation at an intuitive level. What are the root causes of this unit's poor performance? And they *don't* automatically take the easy option: firing the GM and their team. Because the best ODs know that (whilst this might be an issue, some of the time) the issues relating to declining sales might have more systemic problems that need solving (i.e. positioning, product, price, amenity investment, etc.).

- **Right First Time**: I also notice that really great ODs hardly ever feature on company 'shit lists' for not executing company initiatives on time and to specification. Why? Because they explain to their teams the 'what', 'why' and 'how' and get their teams to execute quickly, putting check-back loops in to manage risk and compliance. This then gives them the time and space – having constantly got it right first time – to do 'market share grab' activity and other added value activities.

- **High Expectations**: allied to this, outstanding ODs have extremely high expectations for quality and standards within their businesses. On my CEO visits, I can tell almost immediately who the OD for a particular unit is, because it will bear their 'standards imprint' (good or bad!). They are assiduous at making both unannounced visits (which they feedback to the GM and AM) and accompanied visits with their AMs, where they are particularly good at coaching and reinforcing what their *experiential expectations* are within their region/brand (cleanliness, lighting, music, atmosphere, service delivery, etc.). In short, they treat their regional/brand business as if it were their own personal business with regards to *experiential delivery* and standards!

- *Listen to 'Big Dogs'*: there is also something that many great ODs do that often lies hidden beneath the radar – they recognise who the opinion-former GMs are in their region/brand and open up close channels of dialogue with them. That is not to say that they undermine their AMs. Certainly not. But some of the best ODs have some of their 'big dog' GMs on speed dial so that they can sense check whether certain initiatives will work and take the temperature of morale within the region. This intelligence prevents them from making giant missteps that could lose them the locker room.

- *Leverage Interdependencies*: the final thing – and it often takes a while to master – is an understanding that working with, rather than against, HQ can produce some remarkable outcomes. Too often, ODs actively foster a 'them and us' spirit against their corporate centre (to create their own team bonding); but this is ultimately self-defeating. The interdependencies between the field and the functions (particularly market data analysis and digital sales) are now so great that the best ODs recognise that they cannot and should not attempt to overpower functional experts just because they 'own' the P&L. I demand and expect collaborative relationships between my senior field operators and my functional heads; I can't let toxic relationships and operational bullying breed amongst my wider team. We are stronger when we all work together respectfully. The best ODs get this and are always first in the queue; consequently, they get the best service from the centre!

If those are the standout factors of great ODs, how do they get into the role from Area Manager level? Obviously, in large companies there will be quite a number of high-performing AMs that consistently outperform their peers. How do those that progress truly differentiate themselves? Quite simply – they make a name for themselves! They *become famous for something* in the organisation, above and beyond their Area performance. They provide the inspiration for new products, propositions or ways of working that make a real difference. They become real authorities in certain segments of the market (such as late night, sport or value food), commanding the attention and interest of senior decision-makers within the organisation. And having contributed to the bigger picture and worked collaboratively across the organisation, these star AM performers have put themselves higher up the pecking order to become outstanding ODs of the future!

# CHAPTER ONE

# OD CONTEXT

The preceding case study from Simon Longbottom provides a magnificent overview of the main characteristics of outstanding ODs – starting with their ability to create a 'trench spirit' culture – that will be echoed throughout this book. However, it was not always thus! Starting off in the licensed trade in the mid-1980s, I can well recall the hard-arsed 'barons' who ran their regions for the Big Six national pub companies with iron rods! This changed, with the demands of the OD role in UK licensed food and drink becoming far more intricate over the past thirty years. Why? *First*, the 1990 Beer Orders atomised the Big Six pub operators into smaller (largely) managed enti-ties, releasing thousands of pubs for start-up 'Pub Co's' (Enterprise, Unique, Punch, Admiral, etc.) requiring better commercial skills from ODs. *Second*, many brands and techniques from US food service were imported, presaging the rapid growth of fast-food outlets and a plethora of 'formulaic' informal casual dining concepts. ODs operating in these contexts required more sophisticated technical skills to deliver more complex food-led blueprinted operations. *Third*, the remaining managed pub operators themselves had to adapt to their new competitive environment by creating quality high-street and suburban formats, targeting key consumer demographics and occasions, with ODs requiring far more inspirational, innovative and creative leadership approaches.

Thus, the past thirty years have witnessed a revolution in licensed hospi-tality in the UK, needing senior field leadership with – as Simon Longbottom highlights above – a far higher degree of IQ and EQ. But before we consider the *competencies* and *capability development* mechanisms required for outstanding OD practice, we must address the *industrial* and *organisational* context in which they operate today. Building upon the challenges high-lighted in the Introduction, what barriers do they face and what trends and opportunities can they exploit over the next decade?

# INDUSTRIAL DISRUPTION

As of December 2019, there were 116,000 licensed premises in the UK – including 47,000 pubs – generating £66bn in sales[2]. Then – in early 2020 – the COVID-19 pandemic hit, triggering government-induced closures or capacity restrictions throughout the industry from March 2020 onwards. The effect? By the end of 2020, 12,000 licensed units had been closed permanently. Also, specifically within the pubs sector, 61% of sales were wiped out over the year, with 2,500 sites closing permanently – the worst tally in recent years after a period of relative stabilisation. But what were the consequences of this *apocalyptic meltdown* and – more importantly – what are the *opportunities* for the industry going forwards?

## *APOCALYPTIC MELTDOWN*

It was the ultimate black swan – nobody had seen it coming. A couple of landmark deals were made in the pub sector in late 2019 and early 2020, which marked the high point of confidence. At the time, market belief in the 'freehold-backed' pub sector was returning, as the 'leasehold encumbered' full-service casual dining segment 'bull run' shuddered to a halt (with – most notably – the CVAs of Carluccio's, Byron and Gourmet Burger Kitchen preceding the pandemic). But in March 2020 – for the first time in living memory – the UK government shut down or placed onerous trading restrictions on hospitality throughout the rest of the year and early 2021 in order to slow down COVID-19 viral transmission rates – even though it was estimated that only 3% of infections originated from hospitality establishments (due to their investment in distancing and hygiene mechanisms). Whilst there was government support in the form of furloughed employment payments, VAT relief, HMRC and rental moratoriums, the impact on the industry was monumental, resulting in what I would term the COVID six 'C's:

- **CASHFLOW Squeeze** – in the absence of any (or sporadic) revenue streams, many companies had to refinance their balance sheets (through their banks' or shareholders' discretion), dip into government loan/support schemes, defer HMRC and quarterly rental payments, and cut operational costs down to the bare bones in

---

2   The figures and statistics quoted in these sections are mainly derived from two sources: Lumina Intelligence's 'UK Pub Market Report 2020' (2021) and CGA/Alix Partner's 'Market Growth Monitor Report' (2021).

order to limit their 'cash burn'. The long-term repercussions of this? Unlike supermarket retail, which experienced a pandemic boom, licensed retail will have hangover debts (i.e. onerous borrowing and rental back payments, etc.) that might restrict estate investment and commercial room for manoeuvre well into the future. As a consequence of this, it is likely that companies will focus far more on cashflow generation/preservation going forwards, rather than traditional profit metrics.

- **CATEGORY Collapses** – overleveraged, over-rented 'Zombie' full-service casual dining concepts that were teetering going into the pandemic were either wiped out or – having entered CVAs – restructured with far fewer outlet numbers (i.e. Frankie and Benny's, Pizza Express, etc.). In addition, 'drinks-led' categories (particularly nightclubs and bars) were badly affected by government dictats at various junctures during 2020–21, including: the 'rule of six', 'one-metre' social distancing, bans on 'vertical drinking' at the bar, the linking of alcoholic drink consumption to 'substantial meal' purchases, and the restriction of eating and drinking to outside spaces.

- **CONSUMER Changes** – inevitably, the pandemic rocked consumer economic confidence and consumers' faith in hospitality, with customers citing their main barriers to visiting pubs – when they were sporadically open up until June 2021 – as being: 'the avoidance of crowds' (26%), 'saving money' (14%) and 'cheaper drinks at home' (12%). Nevertheless, when consumers were able to dine inside or outside licensed premises at various times and locations in the UK, they were happy to adopt and use the 'order and pay' apps provided to facilitate service-provider distance. Interestingly, NPS scores relating to customer perceptions of service quality and speed actually increased during these periods – compared to pre-pandemic levels – suggesting that consumers were quite happy with digitally enhanced service cycles that removed a number of irritating bottlenecks!

- **CHANNEL Switches** – the peripatetic closure and/or partial opening of licensed hospitality during 2020 and early 2021 provided a boon for the fast food and online takeaway delivery companies (JustEat, Deliveroo, UberEats, etc.). In February 2021, according to CGA, sales of deliveries and takeaways from leading hospitality groups were 317% on the same month the year before. Also, increased 'digital socialisation' (Zoom parties etc.) boosted supermarket retail alcohol and food sales. Nonetheless, the government-backed 'Eat Out to Help Out' scheme in August 2020 fired up like-for-like sales in the sector, particularly in food-led suburban/residential pubs. To this extent, takeaways, supermarket retail and suburban/residential pubs were the winners during the pandemic.

- **COST Pressures** – having to operate a 'full service' business model requiring extra labour, with restricted capacity and opening hours, meant that many pubs and restaurants were – at best – only able to break even at various junctures during the pandemic (trading at 60–80% of pre-COVID levels). In addition, the costs of making units 'COVID safe', throwing away stock when outlets were closed down and absorbing a NLW increase during the height of the pandemic increased cost pressures on operators. In the future, continued 'COVID-proofing' costs – such as screening, sanitisa-tion, reconfigured seating and zoning, plus enhanced ventilation and air-conditioning systems – will impose further burdens on the industry.

- **CAPABILITY Deficit** – national border lockdowns, bans on inter-national travel and the sheer duration of the crisis – coupled with the fact that many smaller businesses were unable to afford furlough contributions – precipitated the flight of a fair proportion of foreign national labour back to their home countries. Given that, pre-pandemic, EU foreign nationals had accounted for 43% of the wider hospitality sector's workforce (with nearly 70% deployed in demanding kitchen and back-of-house roles), a serious capability deficit loomed – particularly in London and the South East – in the run up to nationwide re-opening in mid-2021. Going forwards, the dual impact of Brexit and COVID will most likely – in spite of outlet closures and overall capacity reductions – lead to severe shortages in skilled labour that will only be ameliorated through significant developmental and remuneratory action by businesses in the short to medium term.

## *TRENDS AND OPPORTUNITIES*

During the dark times of the pandemic, it was very hard for anyone in the hospitality, leisure and tourism industries to imagine a positive future. Furloughing had prevented mass redundancies at the beginning, protecting nearly three million hospitality jobs; but in the end, the pandemic still cost thousands of front-of-house employees and a slew of middle managers their jobs. Countless hospitality companies had been either demolished or diminished by the side-effects of the pandemic, but – following the discovery of vaccines – hope returned. Those still standing (especially freehold-owned pub estates) stood to prosper from the disappearance of a sizable chunk of capacity from the 'in-premise' food-service market, 'staycation trade' and the enticing prospect of huge pent-up consumer demand. So, taking into account the after-effects of COVID, what *trends and opportunities* lie ahead for licensed 'in-premise' hospitality in the UK?

- **SAFE Socialisation** – although memories of the worst excesses of the pandemic will fade, 'COVID panic' – stoked by media reports on virulent variants and cautious government guidelines – will continue to affect consumer behaviour. Fear over 'mixing in crowds' (especially in the over-50 demographic) is sure to continue, resulting in risk-averse customers continuing to 'digitally socialise', keeping away from city centres and packed drinks-led occasions. For certain demographics and portions of the population, 'stay safe' behaviours will govern the actions of many consumers for some time to come, reducing traffic in specific locations and formats.

- **SUBURBAN Growth** – with restrictions on international travel hitting urban tourist hotspots hard and many UK consumers staying local – due to health concerns and a higher proportion of people working from home – which licensed-house business models will be the most successful over the next five years? In all likelihood, suburban and residential based offers – including locally relevant drinks-led community pubs (with a food offer) and destination food pubs with 'optimised' gardens – will prosper most over the short to medium term.

- **STIMULATING Experiences** – prior to the pandemic, the hospitality market had witnessed two powerful trends – premiumisation and a craving for experiential leisure – which are likely to accelerate over the next decade. In terms of premiumisation, consumers traded up the 'brand hierarchy' (favouring M&B's Miller and Carter or Peter Borg-Neil's Oakman Inns), abandoning homogenised value brands (resulting in reductions in outlet numbers for M&B's Sizzling Pubs and Harvester, Whitbread's Brewer's Fayre and Table Table and Greene King's Flaming Grill brand). In terms of 'experiential leisure', many established and start-up companies combined eating and drinking with forms of competitive socialising that enhanced customer experiences (i.e. pub sports, bowling, table tennis, escape rooms, etc.).

- **STRIKING Uniqueness** – allied to this, another consumer trend – a preference for *'heterogeneous uniqueness'* – will also require hospitality operators to address a consumer craving for 'non-corporate' offers. It was striking that pre-pandemic, the top five pub group estates in the UK reduced their number of branded sites by 18%, suggesting that an 'unbranded resurgence' of local, unique pubs (supplied by the likes of the Stonegate Group) – a reaction to faceless, emotionless corporatism – will be a powerful force over the next decade.

- **SCALE Operations** – counterintuitively perhaps, these forces for premiumisation, experiences and uniqueness will need to be accompanied by *scale*. Why? The inexorable rise of fixed and variable costs underpinning the UK food and drink industry (combined with the debts accrued during COVID) mean that only units with 'scalable business models' that can *command higher pricing* to defray more onerous operating costs will flourish during the next decade (even though there will be thousands of 'sub-scale' lifestyle businesses that limp on!). From 2015 to 2020, the top ten pub groups in the UK increased their managed estates from 31% to 45% of their assets. Why? It enabled them to build and operate scale units with greater resources to keep on top of consumer trends, control pricing and execute consistently (producing a quality offer).

- **SHARED Occasions** – over the past fifteen years there has been a sea-change in licensed premises usage. Timeslot traffic has gravitated towards the end of the week – capacity utilisation has been generally low during Monday–Wednesday sessions (with the exception of 'silver fox' lunchtime diners). Shared group occasions, celebratory gatherings and key seasonal events have become more important to operators to sweat their assets during peak trading times. During COVID, for instance, 60% of the 18–24 demographic said that they were put off using pubs by not being able to meet in larger groups of six. The art of exploiting this need for planned (rather than spontaneous) shared occasions will be essential over the coming years.

- **SMART Technology** – in order to facilitate the planning of shared occasions, operators will build upon their learnings from the 'order and pay' apps they hastily adopted (to great effect) during the pandemic. Over the next decade, the winners in this sector will be the ones that have invested in frictionless 'digital service cycle' technology, helping customers locate their website 'portals' to use smooth pre-booking/ordering engines (optimising spend per head), backed up by swift payment and advocacy systems! The 'big data' harvested from this technological goldmine of information will also assist operators in shaping their future offers according to 'real-time' customer behaviours, needs, feelings and preferences. It will also help the industry to exploit key trading sessions more effectively and (simultaneously) reduce the cost of serve!

- **SUSTAINABLE Sourcing** – in addition – particularly to satisfy the millennial demographic – operators will have to bolster their local, 'eco' credentials over the next decade. Where they source ingredients (both plant-based and protein) and how big their carbon footprint is – as the nation switches from fossil fuels to alternative energy – will become greater live issues. Those operators that are able to burnish their 'local' and 'eco-friendly' credentials will ultimately outperform those that ignore the impending ESG (Environmental Social Governance) revolution.

- **SYMPATHETIC Leadership** – over the past five years the mental health and well-being of employees within hospitality has become a more visible and pressing issue. Why? Raising anxiety and stress issues has become less taboo in a new celebrity 'disclosure culture'. Companies will have to invest far more time and resources into supporting employee well-being over the next decade and leaders will have to adopt a far more empathetic, understanding tone to motivate and engage a more 'fragile' workforce.

# ORGANISATIONAL RESHAPING

COVID has severely disrupted the hospitality industry, shaping future macro-trends and opportunities. But what about organisations themselves – how have they responded and what will they look like going forwards? In the Introduction and my previous books on multi-unit leadership[3], I highlighted the archetypal organisational tensions within hospitality chains, including:

---

3   For instance: Edger, C., *Effective Multi-Unit Leadership – Local Leadership in Multi-Site Situations* (London: Routledge, 2012, 2016); Edger, C., *International Multi-Unit Leadership – Developing Leaders in International Multi-Site Operations* (London: Routledge, 2012, 2016); Edger, C., *Professional Area Management – Leading at a Distance in Multi-Unit Enterprises* (Oxford: Libri, 1st ed. 2014, 2nd ed. 2015); Edger, C., and Emmerson, A., *Franchising – How Both Sides Can Win* (Oxford: Libri, 2015); and Edger, C., *Retail Area Management – Strategic and Local Models for Driving Growth* (Oxford: Libri, 2016).

- o *Level of distance* (causing psychological, geographical, functional or structural 'detachment')
- o *Lifecycle position* (start-up 'values-led' mentality vs mature 'bureaucratic' culture)
- o *Field vs centre* (effectiveness pitted against efficiency)
- o *Standardisation vs customisation* ('global' or 'local'?)
- o *Format/channel proliferation* ('multi-velocity' estates).

However, many of these 'peace-time' organisational tensions, battles and contradictions became diluted during COVID, as organisations battled for their very existence. During the 'burning platform' of the pandemic, organisations adapted to their new circumstances, becoming more:

- **Lean** – firstly, to preserve cash, most organisations had to 're-size' and 'downscale' their overheads pretty rapidly. Although furloughing prevented mass lay-offs at unit level earlier on during the pandemic, head-office costs were slashed as expensive central overhead was made redundant. However, as one sector CEO remarked to me at the height of the pandemic, his leaner organisation (with 40% less central resource) was – in his view – twice as productive.

- **Agile** – the fact that the government constantly changed the 'trading goalposts' – often with little warning – meant that organisations became more agile. How? By increasing their responsiveness to new rules and regulations (which varied around the country) by quickening up their decision-making processes; and making snap strategic and operational decisions, requiring instant implementation – increasing their speed to market.

- **Collaborative** – also during the COVID crisis, organisations developed more of a 'one-team' mentality with less friction and gameplay being exhibited between functions and the field. A collaborative 'Dunkirk spirit' prevailed where old enmities and rivalries between 'professional elites' were put aside in pursuit of the collective good.

- **Innovative** – given the restrictions that the sector was placed under at various junctures, operators had to become more innovative and ingenuous as to how they generated trade, converted profit and conserved cash. For instance, the Craft Union format within Stonegate installed pizza ovens to serve 'substantial meals', many pubs started delivery and takeaway services (with M&B reporting record Toby Carvery takeout sales) and opening up totally new channels of business (Pizza Pilgrims' 'Pizza in the Post' initiative being a prime example – see Case Study 2, below). Also, companies became far more adept at using outside trading space, turning precious covers/tables and quickly adopting/exploiting online (multi-channel) booking/ordering/payment systems.

- **Connected** – above all, the industry became more attuned to using digital technology (Zoom, Skype and Microsoft Teams) to communicate internally, with CEOs, MDs and ODs providing regular updates to their people. Perhaps not as effective as face-to-face, but internal engagement surveys consistently showed that regular online briefings from the likes of Phil Urban (CEO, M&B), Nick McKenzie (CEO, Greene King), Simon Longbottom (CEO, Stonegate) and Clive Chesser (CEO, Punch) were regarded as being highly motivational by their people. Externally, companies connected with their local communities by giving away food (that would have perished during successive lockdowns) and providing free meals and delivery services for the needy, old and vulnerable.

As a means of illustrating the points above, the following case study – written at the height of the pandemic by Gavin Smith, Managing Director of Pizza Pilgrims – illustrates the way in which companies and leaders adapted to their new challenges.

*CASE STUDY 2 – HOSPITALITY LOCKDOWN – WHAT HAVE I LEARNT?*
*GAVIN SMITH, MANAGING DIRECTOR, PIZZA PILGRIMS*

My role in leading Pizza Pilgrims has always been fundamentally underpinned by proactive planning 6–12 months ahead with our business, our team and our pizza. Coronavirus has challenged our assumptions for the future but has also identified a myriad of exciting opportunities. There are a small number of principles that guide our thinking here at Pizza Pilgrims.

**Positive support for our team**

- **Choice** – no one has to come to work unless they have personally requested to do so.

- **Support** – we moved every head chef to a salary; we pay *'appreciation'* supplements to those choosing to return to work, we pay a travel contribution for those choosing to return to work; we have made zero redundancies and laid nobody off; and we have also paid a contribution to those not covered by furlough.

## Inclusive communication

- **Adaptation** – we have initiated revised ways of working, enabling us to engage every person, from team members to shareholders. We have welcomed new channels, from Zoom to Facebook workplace, to communicate with all our staff.

- **Fun** – my team have been exceptionally driven to ensuring we stay upbeat and have fun where we can. We have enjoyed everything from pizza cook-a-long classes, family quizzes to sunset beers on Zoom. Having fun has always been key to our ethos and it's crucial we maintain this throughout the strange times we are living in.

- **External comms** – we have communicated as pragmatically as possible, despite the constraints we have faced, to all guests, partners, suppliers and contractors.

## Trading mindset

- **Safety first** – where it is safe to do so and with our team who want to work, we have looked to trade and implemented a very clear set of guidelines for our staff and partners to work safely in a socially distanced manner.

- **Bury the budget** – we are focussed on liquidity and profitable revenue streams even if the margins are not what we had initially planned for. Cash is king and we see the short term as survival.

- **Brand building** – we have exciting and innovative stories and we are protecting the brand, which is incredibly important for us all, long term. If you choose not to trade or not to talk to your followers, you risk a devaluation of the brand.

## Purposeful leadership

- **Style** – stay calm and natural and please don't panic. We have made decisions in smaller groups when we have needed to make things happen fast.

- **Innovate** – where we can, we have adapted our model. This week we went live with our *'pizza in the post'*, which is providing revenue we would not normally have secured, allowing people across the UK to try our amazing Neapolitan pizza. We have also worked closely with Deliveroo in adapting the menu, creating packages and understanding postcode demand for our pizza in every region.

- **Relationships** – we have leaned on our closest partners in business to support our trading and thinking over the last month. I have been inspired by the expertise and the support I have been offered by partners including: Salvo, Moretti (Heineken UK), Deliveroo, Reynolds, Natwest, W Communications, IPW... to name but a few.

**Define the post-coronavirus pizzeria**

- **Social distancing** – this is likely to be here for some time, so we are building and creating to several possible scenarios which will accommodate this new world, with implications for everything from hosting to payment and a whole lot of other stuff in between.

- **Academy** – we will use our Camden academy to define and share changes in the way we intend to do business. We will have succinctly developed and engaging support tools for all our team to help them work effectively in the new world.

- **Menu** – we are working through what adaptations and enhancements we need to make to our food and drinks offer, to ensure we protect value and innovation while ensuring we still have the best pizza for our guests.

- **Charitable work** – we will continue to support the NHS, local charities and hospitality workers in any way that is useful and achievable.

- **Landlords** – much has been written about faceless landlords and the behaviours they have or have not displayed throughout this lockdown. I have to say that we have had great conversations in almost all cases, and we intend to continue an open and honest dialogue with all landlords based on the principle that we should share the benefit and pain.

- **Systems** – we are looking at every system and process we have in place, asking: 'Does this make the pizza better?' or 'Does this enable our teams to deliver a better experience?' We will make changes where necessary.

- **General Manager and Head Chef roles** – we recognise these are some of the most important people in the business. We are looking closely at their roles to see how we can enable them to be more effective and will make changes if we feel they add value.

- **Partners** – we are looking at those who have been useful and helpful throughout this crisis. If they have been neither, we will find more aligned partners before we re-open.

My current conclusion is that our industry is experiencing an unprecedented challenge and this is likely to worsen before it improves. However, we are an industry built on innovation, collaboration and positivity. I intend to focus only on what I can impact, and to prepare our team and business to win in a new and challenging trading environment. I am confident we will be stronger on the other side of this, and we should protect our team and support our industry wherever we can.

# HUMAN DIMENSION

Pre-pandemic, the hospitality sector in the UK afforded abundant career and job opportunities – in spite of a contraction in the full-service casual dining sector. As I have alluded to, after years of closures and 'under-rating' by the City, the pub sector had come back into fashion, with investment being poured into estates. However, in addition to providing significant industrial and organisational disruption to this momentum, COVID also had a dramatic human effect at all levels within the sector. Obviously, during the course of researching this book, I listened at first hand to hopes and fears of senior leaders in the sector about what the short- and long-term effects might be for them personally and professionally. There were some that, at the beginning of the pandemic, privately confessed to me that after years working on the front-line 24/7, an enforced break came as a blessed relief – a respite from chasing demanding financial targets on the hamster wheel of capitalism! But in the main, thoughts and feelings coalesced around the following:

- **Stress** – the predominant feeling amongst respondents was one of *stress* and frustration relating to job security and the future of the industry. Would they have a job at the other end of this? Would hospitality ever return to pre-pandemic levels when the nightmare abated?

- **Bitterness** – also, the furlough system (a government-backed scheme to part-pay 'laid off' workers to prevent redundancies) was viewed as quite *divisive*. Some managers and executives were furloughed throughout the pandemic, others were placed on 'flexi-furlough' and those in the 'core gang' – dealing with business survival – worked the duration of the crisis. Those that were furloughed completely or more frequently than their peers felt bitter about what this signalled about their relative position in the pecking order, when – in their view – inferior personnel were favoured to 'keep the show on the road'. Would they be the next to go if the company needed to cut more roles?

- **Loss** – in addition, several executives had to make some tough decisions, eventually letting go of 'A listers' (in spite of furlough), causing them feelings of bereavement, guilt and regret. They weren't cutting 'dead wood' – they were releasing great people into a jobless market where they would have little or no prospect of finding equivalent paid employment in the short term.

- **Separation** – all senior respondents agreed on one thing: that they missed the face-to-face interaction and camaraderie of their teams and businesses. All good operators derive a great deal of emotional energy from the buzz of front-line field operations. The stop–start nature of the industry during the pandemic led many senior leaders genuinely to suffer from separation anxiety.

- **Burn Out** – finally, those that remained supervising 'lockdown planning' and 'operational fast-response systems', full-time throughout the pandemic, reported feeling 'digitally burnt-out' by March 2021. Not having had a break from the start, staring at a screen for (in some cases) fourteen hours a day – in an isolated home environment – was starting to take a major toll on their well-being.

On a more positive note, enforced breaks and downtime during the pandemic led to self-confessed feelings of:

- **Humility** – an appreciation and awe of how their teams coped with shutting, re-opening and then re-shutting (or offering partial takeaway service) throughout the pandemic. A humble appreciation of the resilience, stoicism and commitment of employees at all levels to try and get their businesses back up and running, abiding by strict government-mandated rules.

- **Reflection** – in addition, enforced time away from the grindstone allowed senior leaders to reflect deeply upon their priorities and aspirations. Some admitted that their lives had previously lacked balance – that they had lost perspective on what was really important to them. To this extent, the pandemic allowed them to reset and refresh their personal goals.

- **Determination** – but overwhelmingly, there was the visceral feeling of determination that they would not let this pandemic herald the demise of their careers, people or businesses. That they would stop at nothing to reignite and reenergise their units coming out of a government-induced 'COVID coma', sensitively transitioning their people to cope and succeed within the new hospitality paradigm.

## SUMMARY

This section has provided *contextual* background to the role of ODs in multi-site hospitality companies – both at present and in the future. Inevitably, given the time of this book's writing, the ravaging effects of the COVID pandemic loom large in any consideration of the current and future industrial, organisational and human dimensions surrounding the OD position. The COVID crisis totally disrupted hospitality in the UK during the period 2020–2021, decimating businesses and destroying livelihoods. But – as Gavin Smith stated in Case Study 2 – the industry will rise again, arguably wiser and stronger. The COVID six 'C's (*cashflow squeeze, category collapses, consumer changes, channel switches, cost pressures* and *capability deficit*) will affect operators' room for manoeuvre for some time to come but – for those businesses still standing – immense opportunities beckon. The 'Darwinian clear out' of the sector will afford extra expansionary space to those that exploit future trends and opportunities: *safe socialisation, suburban growth, stimulating experiences, striking uniqueness, scalability, shared occasions, smart technology, sustainable sourcing* and *sympathetic leadership approaches*. Furthermore, organisations that emerge from the ashes of the pandemic will be more *lean, agile, collaborative, innovative* and *connected*, and led by a leadership cadre with greater *humility, perspective* and *determination*. But – to get back to the main enquiry of this book – what are the main *competencies* of outstanding ODs and which *capability*-development mechanisms should be deployed to grow and nurture them? These will now be considered – in turn – over the next two sections. Read on!

**CHAPTER TWO**

# OD ROLE, COMPETENCIES AND PRACTICES

Drawing upon the questionnaire and case-study research for this book, what is the scope of the multi-site hospitality *OD role*? More importantly for aspirant and existing ODs and their developers, what are the main *OD competency* requirements – in rank order – that lead to truly *outstanding practice and performance*?

## OD ROLE

ODs, sometimes known as Retail Directors, Regional Directors, Business Directors or Regional Vice-Presidents, are senior field leaders – usually reporting to an MD or CEO – who have P&L responsibility for a region or brand with a denominated number of Area Manager direct reports covering a set number of units. It is often (wrongly) perceived as being a 'superannuated AM/BDM' position, but significant differences exist between the two roles (hinted at in the Introduction), namely greater:

- Portfolio scale
- P&L accountabilities
- Distance from units/customers
- Impact upon shaping the region/brand 'micro-culture'
- Planning horizons (manpower, budgeting, investment and marketing)
- Authority/sign-off powers
- Strategic influence
- Central involvement
- Change-management responsibilities.

Given the step up in requirements and the increased complexity of the role, what should the *optimum OD spans of control* and *portfolio size* be? Furthermore, what differing types of *business models* do they lead and *how should their leadership approaches* correspondingly fit?

## *SPANS OF CONTROL*

The overwhelming view of questionnaire respondents was that the optimal number of AM direct reports that ODs could cope with was eight.

- **Why the 'Rule of Eight'?**

> Eight gives you enough flex to bring newbies and junior managers through…
>
> Scott Fowler, Operations Director, Whitbread Restaurants

> Eight is the right size to enable quicker decision-making and buy-in…
>
> John Dyson, National Operations Director, Mecca Bingo

> Beyond eight, you don't get enough contact – you can't speak to them or give enough guidance.
>
> Elton Gray, Operations Director, Creams Café

> Eight is optimal – if you have more and (say) four with performance issues, it gets painful very quickly!
>
> Ric Fyfe, Operations Director, Gather and Gather

- **Exceptions to the Rule of Eight** – however, exceptions to the 'Rule of Eight' did exist according to respondents, according to the operational complexity of the offer (value or premium), economic scale of the units (£6k or £50k per week takings?), concept/brand lifecycle (early start-up 'values' stage or mature 'manual' phase), culture (entrepreneurial versus compliance-led) and ownership type (local family/regional versus corporate). Offer complexity, unit scale, early lifecycle, a 'soft' culture and benign ownership type often resulted in a reduction of OD–AM spans of control to four-to-six direct reports.

## *OPTIMAL PORTFOLIO SIZE*

Ideal OD portfolio sizes were determined by respondents as being *120–140 units for Managed Formats* (with an upper limit of 15 units per AM) and *300 for Leased and Tenanted Formats* (with a maximum of 35–45 units per BDM).

- **Why should OD portfolio sizes have an upper limit?**

> A major test for a managed house OD's portfolio size is whether they can manage to learn the names of all their General Managers and Assistants...
>
> Adrian Frid, National Operations Director, Caffè Nero

> If you go beyond a certain number of managed units, you sacrifice your degree of presence and connectivity...
>
> Jon Walters, Operations Director, Qbic Hotels

> Competent ODs in L&T can handle a portfolio size of 300 with eight BDMs – most of the estate should 'self-manage' (if it is set up properly) but the OD must gain intimate knowledge of the tail (which requires churn), sites that could benefit from expansionary capital and the requirements of their prominent multi-site operators...
>
> Clive Chesser, CEO, Punch Pubs & Co

- **When and why should there be exceptions from the norm?**
  - o **Operational Complexity** – for example, ODs running premium managed units (incorporating complex service and food delivery systems) require smaller portfolio sizes, compared to ODs in 'grab and go' value-led operations because:

27

Running premium managed units requires maintaining high levels of customer intimacy and complex menu delivery; in order to deliver a high-end quality experience (commanding a high price), ODs should only (ideally) be responsible for up to 100 units...

Martin Nelson, Operations Director, Premium Country Pubs (Mitchells and Butlers)

o **Economic Scale** – ODs running a portfolio of battleship units (taking in excess of £4m per annum) need smaller spans of control because:

40 sites maximum for ODs (with a maximum of six AMs running seven sites each) is the optimal number if you are trying to grow units taking more than £4m in sales a year! You can only build capability in these huge businesses by leaving flex in the system for the OD and their AMs – you have to give the OD the time and scope to refresh the talent bank if you want to grow the business. Optimisation is more important than maximisation...

Doug Wright, CEO, Wright Restaurants T/A McDonald's Restaurants

o **Lifecycle Stage** – in addition, ODs operating portfolios in smaller, newly founded, fast-growing operations can only handle a smaller number of units because:

In the early stages of brand/chain development you don't have a manual to standardise operations – you make it up as you go along! Therefore, you've got to be close to operations. Also, as a member of the Executive Team in these start-ups, you will spend a disproportionate amount of time with the owners and investors, seeking alignment and commonality of purpose...

Gavin Smith, Managing Director, Pizza Pilgrims

o **Culture** – the prevailing culture of the organisation will also have a contingent effect on the size of the OD's portfolio:

If you take Stonegate – with its sales-driven entrepreneurial culture – we generally assign 15 units per AM. Why? Unlike other operators who assign greater spans of control to their AMs, we expect our AMs to get to know their sites intimately, driving sales and 'market share grabs' in a creative and dynamic manner!

Helen Charlesworth, Executive Managing Director, Stonegate Group

- o **Ownership type** – finally, the type of owner (corporate plc, private equity, independent/family owned) can also have an impact on OD spans of control:

As an OD in a family brewer, you will sometimes have responsibilities that go beyond just the line (say commercial, machines, HR). This means that your capacity is constrained and – additionally – you will often be simultaneously running both managed and L&T estates, complicating the matter! But generally, family/regional brewers prefer smaller spans of control for ODs so that they can 'wrap their arms' around their estate.

Stephen Gould, Managing Director, Everards

The implications of what the interviewees stated above are clear: *sub-optimal OD–AM spans of control and portfolio sizes = sub-optimal OD performance!* Therefore, OD portfolio architecture design must take into account factors such as offer complexity, unit economic scale and lifecycle positioning if ODs are to perform effectively. Furthermore, the respondents all agreed on another thing – 'span breakers' are a bad idea. Commonly, organisations try to manage OD workloads by introducing direct report 'span breakers' (usually called 'Operations Managers') who assume responsibility for three-to-four AM/BDMs in order to relieve the OD burden. This was universally seen as a bad idea by respondents as it increased the risk of *'splintering'* (creating unnecessary divisions within the tribe).

# DIFFERING BUSINESS MODEL REQUIREMENTS

Any analysis of what constitutes outstanding OD practice has to start with a recognition that *different hospitality business models* require different 'nuanced' OD approaches for optimal success. But what were the views of the respondents for the differing approaches and requirements for ODs that ran each of the various formats?

- **Unbranded Managed Formats** – the consensus of the twenty-seven questionnaire respondents was that ODs of Unbranded Managed Formats should adopt a **'street-fighter mentality'** which encompassed: 'looseness (within defined parameters), nimbleness, creative thinking, open support networks, flexibility, agility, customisation, bottom-up innovation, pragmatism, entrepreneurship, high level of local responsiveness, etc.'

ODs of unbranded managed formats have to trust people by giving them freedom within a fixed frame. They also need to encourage and facilitate a culture of best practice sharing, implementing the best added-value ideas across their portfolio quickly to gain local competitive advantage. But fundamentally, they need a 'streetfighter' mentality! Every micro-market is exploitable, every competitor can be overcome and every relevant consumer occasion can be maximised! Optimism, proactivity, aggression, creativity and flexibility are the main characteristics of successful ODs in this business model.

Colin Hawkins, Divisional Operations Director, Stonegate
Group

- **Single Managed Brand Formats** – ODs leading single managed brand formats should – according to the interviewees – adopt a **'monomaniacal mindset'** exemplified by: 'tightness, clarity, focus, grip, rigour, unrelenting consistency, discipline, implementation, execution, etc.'

ODs of single-brand formats require monomaniacal focus to deliver the brand promise and standards. Why? Because it's easy to get distracted running a hospitality brand; multiple priorities can drown the OD but, in the end, they have to run the brand as if it were their own business with ruthless attention to detail that will create exceptional customer experiences time and again...

Karen Forrester, ex-CEO, TGI Fridays

- **Multi-branded Managed Formats** – in contrast, ODs that led multi-branded managed formats needed to take a **'chameleon approach'** which encompassed: 'guardianship of sacred brand differentiators/identities, preventing convergence/homogenisation, applying deft matrix management skills, ambidexterity, etc.'

ODs of multi-branded portfolios need to train their efforts upon maintaining the distinctive differences between their brands. To that extent (and I found this at Strada), you need to be able to adopt a chameleon style in order to 'flip' your style, behaviour and approach between brands. You must be careful that you don't blow the individual brand cultures up by not knowing the vernacular, terminology or detail of the individual service systems...

Elton Gray, Commercial and Operations Director, Creams Café

- **Leased and Tenanted Unbranded Formats** – however, it was accepted that ODs running leased and tenanted unbranded formats required a different approach from their managed counterparts. Given that most of their interactions were with autonomous small business owners (rather than salaried employees), they had to adopt more of a **'negotiating style'** encompassing: 'relationship/trust building, pragmatic win–win solutions, mutual commercial success, reciprocity, collaboration, local market 'fit', etc.'

ODs running leased and tenanted estates need to have broad commercial knowledge, allied to an adaptable, flexible, pragmatic mindset. Once the deal has been signed, you can't tell tenants or lessees what to do – you have to build trusting relationships quickly, which enable you to negotiate and collaborate on forging win–win outcomes…

Mike O'Connor, Operations Director, Greene King Pub Partners

- **Single-Brand Franchised Formats** – finally, ODs leading single-brand franchised formats – where the blueprint has been clearly delineated (with potential breaches, skimming or 'freeriding' threatening brand dilution) – required more of a **'policeman approach'** characterised by: 'brand protection, system expertise, blueprint coaching, compliance, conformance, enforcement, honesty, transparency, etc.'

As an OD, clearly you need to police the blueprint with franchisees. Any dilution or deviation will destroy its credibility in the eyes of the consumer (who has bought into it because of its quality, consistency and dependability). However, what I found when I was running Planet Hollywood franchises was that it was absolutely key to build strategic alliances with franchisees. Why? Often it is easy to fall out over money; you have to build trust and fairness into the economic relationship – standing by your promises – so that you can navigate a way through disputes as and when they arise…

Ric Fyfe, Operations Director, Gather and Gather

The obvious implication of the above findings is that different hospitality business models require different leadership approaches. The knock-on effect of this is that developers, recruiters and aspirant ODs need to be cognisant of the following:

- **Transitioning ODs between some business models might be problematic:**
  - Moving ODs from Managed to L&T (and vice versa) is problematic because the technical skills and leadership styles required for single-branded managed formats

('monomaniacal focus') are considerably different to the 'negotiator' bias of leased and tenanted formats. 'Direct and tell' managed ODs will experience huge kickback in collab-orative/relationship L&T environments. Stripped of their coercive/positional power, they had better learn the dark arts of influencing without (absolute) authority – through relational or expert power resources – or they will be highly likely to fail!

- **Similar business model types ease OD transitions:**
  - o On the other hand, single-brand to multi-brand managed transitions (and vice versa) are possible if transitioning ODs are able to compartmentalise and direct their 'monoma-niacal' focus upon each one of their distinctive brands (to prevent convergence/homogenisation).
  - o Also, single managed brand ODs can be well suited to fran-chised format transitions (their attributes of unrelenting focus upon execution and consistency being particularly useful) if they can also recognise that they need to hone their 'commercial alliance' skills (i.e. ensuring the 'profit pig' is equally divided to serve the interests of fairness and equity).

## CASE STUDY 3 – THE PIVOTAL ROLE OF THE OPERATIONS DIRECTOR

*Clive Chesser is the CEO of Punch Pubs & Co (1,300 leased pubs with a corporate headcount of 250, including an operational field structure of one MD, five ODs and 45 BDMs). Previously, Clive was OD and then MD of Greene King Pub Partners, following spells at Enterprise Inns as an OD and Häagen-Dazs Cafes as International Franchise Director.*

When I was approached to contribute to this book, it suddenly struck me! Why has nothing been written about this position before? After all – in my view – the OD position is the most pivotal role in every multi-unit leisure enterprise. To use a footballing metaphor: the *CEO is the Manager,* your *CFO is the goalkeeper,* your *Executive Team marshal the defence* and your *BDMs (certainly in Leased and Tenanted) are your strikers,* scoring commercial goals upfront. But your *ODs?* They are the *attacking mid-fielders* linking the whole team together and – using a transfer-fee analogy – they command the highest terms, because (ultimately) *their midfield quality* (taking the ball from the back and creating scoring opportunities for the BDMs up front) is what will determine your success!

To my mind, there are three types of OD:

- *Impact Players* – the first set are really glorified Operations Managers. They have wider stakeholder skills than BDMs/Area Managers and are ruthlessly commercial. They hit the numbers. But they fail to build and stretch the strategic capability and skill set of their team. They are great at short-term commercial fixes, but poor at ensuring long-term business sustainability.

- *People-focused Operators* – the second set get results through their people, creating sustainability through building a solid talent base. But sometimes, these ODs (because of excessive people centricity) are commercially underpowered. When crises hit, they can be slow to react and take the tough decisions required, for fear of upsetting people.

- *Holistic Leaders* – the third set have it all. They have *commercial nous*, *inspirational leadership qualities* and possess a *long-term strategic mindset*. They can jog and chew gum! They can articulate where their business will be in three years' time, create a *'winning culture and mentality'* and possess the agility to innovate in order to get there. They seek out new methods of doing things (i.e. different agreement types, investing in viable new trends and formats, etc.) which gives them the competitive edge over their peers.

But being an OD is a tough job. There are two principal qualities that the best have, namely:

- *Stamina* – being an OD is exhausting. At any one time, you might have eight BDMs and the centre firing problems at you. You feel that you will never get to the end of the day with what you are being asked and tasked to do. So you need immense stamina and determination to win. In short, you need to be physically and mentally fit to do the role to a high standard.

- *Authenticity* – being your true self is even more important here than at the AM/BDM level. Why? There are far more people watching – interpreting signs and signals from you on a daily basis. If you put on a mask and it slips, you lose trust. But being authentic and genuine, in the way you behave towards others, enables people to believe in you. Admitting that you don't know everything and showing a little vulnerability makes you human. And people follow authentic humans rather than robots!

If I am totally honest, I don't think I have done a more demanding role during the course of my business career. The final secret to the survival and success of outstanding ODs? They recruit and retain great people! Talent gravitates towards them and they actively nourish and grow it. Regional field teams will only be as strong as their weakest – rather than best – operators. It is their ability to *strategically and commercially* leverage the talents of all their team that sets outstanding ODs apart from the rest.

# OD COMPETENCIES AND PRACTICES

Having briefly looked at the scope of the OD role and its 'nuanced' differences according to business-model type, it would be appropriate to ask whether or not – given its various shades of grey – it can be assigned identifiable generic competencies that define its success. The answer – quite emphatically – is yes! Whilst the OD role requires differing levels of tacit knowledge and stylistic approaches according to business-model context, the fundamental *behavioural, cognitive and technical characteristics that underpin outstanding OD performance* are – as our respondents agreed – generic to all OD roles (with varying emphases). But what competencies – defined as *'the underlying characteristics of a person which result in effective and/or superior performance in a job'* – do ODs need to be successful in the role? Which ones did my research exercise establish to be the most important?

As stated, having drawn upon the views and research of my students on my postgraduate Multi-Unit Leadership programmes (mostly Area Managers who are led by ODs!) and consulted an expert panel of five 'notables', I compiled a list of nine main competencies that were most strongly correlated to outstanding OD practice. I then interviewed twenty-seven CEOs, MDs and ODs from multi-site hospitality (predominantly from the pub sector) using a structured questionnaire (see Figure 1) and asked them to select the top three competencies they believed to be required for outstanding OD practice. The competencies picked with the most frequency – in rank order (from

1–9) – were:

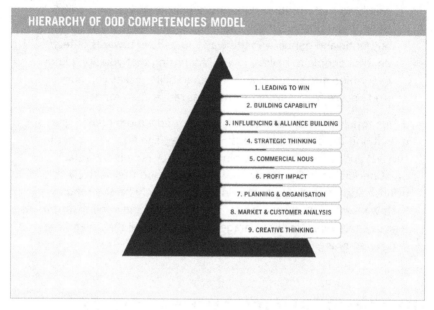

**Figure 2: Hierarchy of Outstanding Operations Director (OOD) Competencies**

What are we to deduce from this order of hierarchy? First, the respondents highlighted **behavioural 'input' focused competencies** (*Leading to Win, Building Capability and Influencing and Alliance Building*) above all others. Why? Because hospitality businesses exist to delight customers with warm, uplifting experiences provided by highly motivated staff with engaging service personalities – which in turn leads to superior site performance. Outstanding ODs provide *inspiring leadership*, creating *vibrant regional/brand cultures* which provide the *right climate* to make this happen. Second, the next three competencies (*Strategic Thinking, Commercial Nous and Profit Impact*) are largely **cognitive competencies** – requiring a great deal of thinking and problem-solving capability. Third, the final three competencies (*Planning and Organisation, Market and Customer Analysis and Creative Thinking*) are important **technical competencies** – but, as one respondent remarked, 'can be facilitated or done by other experts within the organisation.' The implications of these clusterings? Outstanding ODs must have the behavioural (EQ) attributes to lead, but these must be backed by cognitive (IQ) thinking capabilities.

Most remarkable, however, was the correlation of this rank order of outstanding ODs' competencies with the top three differences between the

Area Manager and OD roles cited by the respondents: *Inspirational Leadership, Influencing and Alliance Building*, and *Strategic Thinking*. What are we to make of this? The top-ranked outstanding OD competencies were seen to have the biggest divergence with the Area Manager role, a finding that has profound implications for the development and performance of ODs. Clearly, if aspirant ODs and their developers want them to bridge the chasm between the two roles, they have to clearly understand, digest and work hard on developing the top four competencies – at least – to operate at this level. In short, *they need to transition AMs from a predominantly managerial to a leadership mindset.*

This section will now outline – using quotes and case studies from the inter-viewees – the reasons *why* each competency is so important for outstanding OD performance and *how* outstanding ODs bring them alive by highlighting three practices per competency. Prior to this, however, it is worth considering Adam Fowle's reflections on the competencies of outstanding Operations Directors.

## CASE STUDY 4 –THE COMPETENCIES OF OUTSTANDING OPERATIONS DIRECTORS

*Adam Fowle was Senior Non-Executive Director of the Ei Group (4,400 leased, tenanted and managed pubs) until its sale in February 2020. Previously, he was Chairman of Tesco Hospitality, Non-Executive Director of Bistrot Pierre, CEO of Mitchells and Butlers, the Retail Director of Sains-bury's and Executive Director, Bass Leisure (where he founded Hollywood Bowl).*

When I look back at the traits, characteristics and skills of outstanding ODs that have worked for me over the years, there have been certain commonalities amongst the best.

- **Inspiring Leadership** – great ODs inspire their direct reports and wider regional/brand teams to exert higher levels of discretionary effort than their peers. Why? They *create excellent workplace climates where people help one another out in a common cause.* Yes – they are absolutely insistent upon the highest levels of stand-ards and don't dither with serial underperformance – but they build *collegiate relationships* within their teams based on trust. They also have a great sense of humour which disarms and draws people towards them.

- **Bench Strength** – outstanding ODs create great strength in depth in their regions/brands. They drill down beneath AM/GM levels, connecting with and *nurturing talent* at Assistant, Deputy or Kitchen Management level. They understand that the best GMs are most likely to be 'homegrown' talent that understands the culture of their brand/region and has a thorough insight into its key systems, procedures and ways of working.

- **Productive Central Relationships** – outstanding ODs are also able to *mobilise and energise* the central teams behind them. This aspect is probably the most pivotal difference between the OD and AM role! The capacity to create mutuality and reciprocity with key functional stakeholders (who don't necessarily report into them) is a higher-order skill requiring empathy and diplomacy.

- **Forensic Planning and Organising** – great ODs have an incredibly *methodical* and forensic approach to planning. They have always thought at least 6–12 months ahead; devising people, product and investment plans that they believe will grow the business. Additionally, they also have formidable *project planning* skills that bring these plans to fruition.

- **Obsessive Customer Focus** – they also have what I would describe as a 'laser-eyed view' of the customer. Outstanding ODs 'get' their customer demographics – their desires, feelings and aspirations. This enables them to *thoughtfully* respond to the needs of their customer base with relevant propositions that are properly priced, with the 'correct dialling' on experience, atmosphere and ambience.

- **Asset Optimisation** – they are also smart about how they maximise their property portfolio – getting their hands on capital for either maintenance or expansionary purposes. And most crucially, they really understand the economic and mathematical distinction between the two! Also, they are able to distinguish between asset and human problems. Sometimes capital is required to fire up an asset; often the quicker solutions might lie on the human side of things.

And poor ODs? They usually:

- *Lack leadership skills* – relying on excessive 'managerialism' to 'tick the boxes'

- *Fail to confront poor performance* – accepting excuses in the vain hope that things will magically turn themselves around

- *Display a lack of urgency* – standing back rather than energetically stepping in to sort out issues or land key priorities

- *Have a 'smarts' deficit* – they are really intellectually and cognitively underpowered to do the job, which is a significant step up from the AM role (involving higher levels of complexity and ambiguity).

In summary, outstanding ODs have the emotional and intellectual intelligence to do a demanding role which receives intense corporate scrutiny. How do you develop them? Aside from putting them through strawberry-patch roles (with a smaller number of AM reports and units) and stretching executive education, the best way – in my view – is giving them exposure to the corporate centre (through projects or functional role placements) so that you expand their horizons beyond their AM district 'silos'. Giving them an appreciation of the 'whole game' makes them less insular and more appreciative of the talents and contributions of others before they step up. Because they will need all the help that they can get when they eventually transition into the role!

# #1 LEADING TO WIN

The most important competency that outstanding ODs master – ranked *first* by the twenty-seven questionnaire respondents – is Leading to Win. That is to say they develop the ability to inspire, galvanise and motivate their immediate and indirect reports, *creating a dynamic, proactive culture* – in both benign and adverse circumstances. In the pursuance of doing so, they exhibit self-awareness, mental toughness[4], adaptability, humility,

---

4  Of course, the underlying requirement for this competency is the capability to 'lead oneself!' Namely, being equipped with the requisite *self-awareness, mental toughness* and *installed capacity* to conduct honest, *positive 'internal conversations'* with yourself that will put you in the right frame of mind to lead others. For wider reading on developing a leader 'growth mindset' (whatever the 'situational position'), see 'Coaching Leaders to Raise Self-Awareness', 'Coaching Leaders to Build Mental Toughness', 'Coaching Leaders to Increase Capacity' and 'Coaching Leaders to Adjust Style' in Edger, C., and Heffernan, N., *Advanced Leader Coaching – Accelerating Personal, Interpersonal and Business Growth* (Oxford: Libri, 2020), pp. 17–88.

credibility and confidence, alongside infectious optimism, humour and cultural intelligence.

It isn't easy, however. Manifestly caring about their people and 'giving something of themselves to others' in order to create a *positive working climate* involves making a conscious emotional investment – something that poor ODs singularly fail to do:

> Poor ODs – in my view – usually have four inter-related issues. *First*, they have a one-dimensional view, narrowly focussing upon costs or marketing. *Second*, they don't get the balance right between inputs and outputs; I spend 75% of my time on inputs (culture, people, operations and customers) – poor ODs spend 75% of their time on outputs (P&L and costs – what comes out of the machine). *Third*, they practise what I call 'fake engagement' – they are blind (in Johari Window terms) to their actual effect on people; they think they're amazing but they're not! *Fourth*, they are extremely selfish and lack empathy – they are happy to exhaust their team by constantly withdrawing from their emotional bank accounts...
>
> Colin Hawkins, Divisional Operations Director, Stonegate Group

The reasons why some ODs fall short in this regard might be related to their personality, excessive workload pressures, the way they are being led themselves and/or the overarching (negative) culture of the organisation. However, one of the main explanations why some ODs fail to master this competency is that many – coming from Area Management positions – have underestimated the key 'leadership distinctions' between the two roles:

> For me, 'Leading to Win' is the key difference between the two roles. At Area Manager level, you will largely '*manage*' but as an OD you need an *uplifting leadership style* that fits a larger, distant group of people. With 3,000 people, I need to become more things to more people – I have to work harder to leave a *cultural imprint* over a greater distance. You need to understand your capacity and limitations to achieve that!
>
> Martin Nelson, Operations Director, Premium Country Pubs
> (Mitchells and Butlers)

Clearly – as Martin Nelson observes – greater detachment from day-to-day operations creates a formidable barrier to making a positive *leadership* impact upon the behaviour and performance of their people. So, how do outstanding ODs overcome this hurdle in order to 'Lead to Win'? By practising three things better and more frequently than their peers, namely: *inspiring communications*, *motivational recognition* and *values-based leadership* to create a *vibrant regional/brand culture*. These practices will be considered in turn.

## INSPIRING COMMUNICATIONS

Outstanding ODs communicate clearly and inspirationally – cutting through to the field front-line, making a positive, lasting impression by:

> Being authentic and uplifting in front of their people during planning sessions, meetings and conferences – restaurants can have great systems but they're no good unless they're buzzing with enthusiasm… The best ODs interpret employee surveys to understand how to stop demotivating people or have 'open wrap sessions' where they ask 'tell us about three things that matter to you most that we must fix in the next month'… outstanding ODs are superb two-way communicators – constantly making people feel valued, trusted and special… a 'highway or my way' approach doesn't wash today.
>
> Doug Wright, CEO, Wright Restaurants T/A McDonald's

By contrast, lacking courage and patently feeling the heat from above, lazy ODs:

> Practise transactional rather than transformational communication. What do I mean by this? They are over-corrective and non-protective. For instance, they will take poor messages and 'commands' from their boss (Divisional MD or CEO) and just pass it down the line unfiltered. Great ODs convert messages well and 'divert sewage'. They protect everyone else from feeling the pain, whilst finding a way to win!
>
> Alex Ford, Managing Director, Oakman Inns

However, outstanding ODs – in addition to Doug Wright's observations above – engender trust, pride and organisational momentum through:

- **Cascading the**:
    - o *Right messages* ('how *I will reduce interference* to make your jobs easier!', performance updates, change initiatives, recognition announcements, etc.) to the…
    - o *Right people* (opinion formers, 'big dogs' and 'rain makers') at the…
    - o *Right level* (AM, GM, unit teams) through the…
    - o *Right channels* (digital, face-to-face, social media, conferences, etc.) at the…
    - o *Right time* (targeted rather than scattergun).
- **Furthermore, the content and tone of their communications is**:
    - o *Growth focused*, helpful, value-added, inspiring, clear, positive, authentic, trustworthy, informative, consistent, humorous and optimistic (always with an eye to addressing the fundamental questions for recipients, namely: *'what's in it for me?'* and *'how does this effect my job?'*, etc.).

These elements are illuminated and highlighted by the following case study.

*CASE STUDY 5 – AUTHENTICALLY COMMUNICATING IN PREMIUM PUBS*

*Martin Nelson is the Operations Director of the Premium Country Pubs brand, owned by Mitchells and Butlers (with 120 pubs, 3,000 employees, one Operations Manager and eleven Area Managers). Previously, Martin had other senior field roles with other brands and is a 2013 graduate of BCU's MSc in Multi-Unit Leadership Programme (with distinction).*

It is vital that ODs get the *tone and content* of their communications right. Unlike Area Managers, who have day-to-day contact with their GMs and Units, ODs are one step further removed; they have to work harder to make sure the *clarity and purpose* of their communication is on point. Having led both value and premium brands, communications also need to be more *nuanced* in premium contexts. What do I mean by that? In *value brands*, your audience is generally much older and expects a more *directive* style. In *premium* brands with a much younger demographic, who are well educated with extremely high aspirations, you have to adopt a more *inspirational, explanatory* approach to build a more *'inclusive culture'*. In these contexts, it is essential that you really do communicate a *higher sense of purpose* and explain the *'why'*, because if you don't, you will lose their hearts and minds.

So, what is my *philosophy* regarding how I communicate in premium branded contexts?

- ***Accuracy*** – the first thing is that your communications as an OD have to be *well planned and organised*. *Formal* communications regarding initiatives (seasonal events, menu/drinks rotations, etc.), changes (policies and procedures), brand performance (customers, margins, sales, profit, investment ROIs, etc.) need to be cascaded by briefings through the levels (AM–GM–House Teams) or at my twice-yearly 'Comms Forums'. There are also company-generated announcements (such as quarterly results etc.) that need to be fed down through the channels. But the key point is this: important business-led information needs to be *timely, clear and accurate*.

- ***Accessibility*** – but events move quickly in brands like ours, where the consumer need for innovation and originality runs high. To that end, we have brand, district and key 'sub-group' (i.e. bar, kitchen, sales) Facebook 'hubs' where we can directly communicate with our people in real time and they can have *spontaneous conversations* with one another. In addition, we also have a team-member app, which enables individuals to communicate and swap information with colleagues. However, the expectation in premium contexts – quite unlike value-led ones, where there is quite a high degree of reverence and deference – is that I should be *open, accessible and answerable* to all of my people! If something popular has been landed, my millennials will contact me direct over social media and digital channels to tell me. Conversely, if something has deflated their mood and motivation – they won't shy away from telling me directly what they think. The downside of this is that I am at the 24/7 mercy of my people; but the value to me is that I can *gauge the temperature* and act quickly to rectify things if necessary.

- **_Authenticity_** – in terms of the content I post to our wider teams, I am a great fan of making emotional connections that focus upon creating great experiences and memories for our guests. I don't subscribe to the view that, as an OD, I should post a load of stuff regarding figures and financials. My job is to rally the team – set the dynamic tone and purpose, in keeping with the informal nature of the brand. My style is quite humorous and low key, rather than hectoring and loud! Stylistically, I like to post videos with other members of my team (GMs and team members) that show us doing and talking about things that are meaningful.

An example of where I think my philosophy and approach bore fruit occurred when we combined PCDG (Premium Country Dining Group) and VPK (Village Pub and Kitchen) together to form Premium Country Pubs (PCP) a couple of years ago. Both brands had their own distinctive cultures – PCDG, with bigger sites and higher levels of investment, had a _soft 'guest centric'_ culture, whilst VPK, with its smaller sites and limited funding, had a _hard 'commercially focused'_ culture. In essence, both cultures were the antithesis of one another and – in reality – they despised one another! The way I resolved this – after a quite rocky start – was to get the people from both entities to _respect_ the inherent strengths of one another. How? Essentially, by getting the loudest people on both sides of the fence to go away together for a few days and _communicate_ with one another. Having built up trust and mutual understanding, we were then able to _meld the cultures_ together for PCP, leveraging the best of both: _'guest centricity with a commercial edge!'_ But the point is this: if I had been directive, rather than _inclusive_, the two brands would have taken far longer to merge into one, with a far greater number of casualties (probably including me!) along the way.

So, in summary, in a premium branded context, an _informal, inclusive and participative_ approach to communications works best. Where I have seen ODs go wrong in the past is when they have failed to alter their style to 'fit' the positioning and demographic of the brand. But trying to be _accurate, accessible and authentic_ seems to have worked for me, leading the premium end of M&B's country-pub estate over the last six years.

## *MOTIVATIONAL RECOGNITION*

Alongside uplifting communications and encouraging an 'inclusive culture' (as Martin Nelson outlines above), outstanding ODs practise motivational recognition[5]. That is to say, they excite, animate and bring joy to achievers in their region/brand by tangibly recognising their efforts. Why is this important?

> Ultimately, as an OD you need to be conscious that – for a large part – you are leading a team on minimum wage… therefore, you have to be adept at getting people to unleash discretionary effort… if you can't do that, you will struggle to succeed… in order to build emotional bank accounts – that you can draw upon in tough times – *you need to recognise brilliant behaviours and performance at all levels frequently*… it is the one way you can connect with people and transparently demonstrate that you care about the lengths that some of your NLW people go to make our customers happy.
>
> Colin Hawkins, Divisional Operations Director, Stonegate Group

Inevitably, the organisations they work in will have formal reward and recognition systems (annual/quarterly awards, salary supplements, extra holiday allowances, free meals, vouchers, etc.) that the OD can deploy through their AMs and GMs. But what separates the best from the rest is the way in which outstanding ODs elevate and inspire people, personally recognising outstanding performance through:

- **Planned spontaneity**
    - o Catching people doing it right!
    - o Face-to-face 'surprise' recognition during unit visits
- **Creating memories that boost tribal bonding, self-esteem and social standing**
    - o Celebrating success together (regional/brand award ceremonies)

---

5   On motivating employees, see 'Coaching Leaders to Motivate Employees' in Edger, C., and Heffernan, N., *Advanced Leader Coaching – Accelerating Personal, Interpersonal and Business Growth* (Oxford: Libri, 2020), pp. 113–24.

o Taking photographs of the celebratory moment and posting them on regional/brand social-media accounts (so that recipients can show off to their peers, friends and family)

- **Cheerleading skills and competency acquisition**
  o Specifically recognising those that have increased their capability through training and development.

## CASE STUDY 6 – TRANSFORMATIONAL RECOGNITION

*Helen Charlesworth is the Executive Managing Director of Stonegate's Managed Pubs and Bars businesses (circa 700 units, eight brands/ formats, 12,000 employees, seven Operations Directors and 48 Area Managers). An award-winning senior field operator of over twenty years' experience, Helen was previously Managing Director of Your Move and National Operations Director of Pizza Express.*

Great ODs realise that in order to create an indelible *footprint* within their brand/region, they have to work hard to close down the psychological distance between themselves and their people. Operating across a wide span of control – covering 100–150 units – they have to make their *emotional mark* through rewarding and recognising outstanding behaviours! And they can't just outsource this activity to their AMs. Why? Because behaviour breeds behaviour; publicly acknowledging good practice or 'extra mile' performance *creates a positive culture* – mobilising the right behaviours *right across* their region/brand. Their job – as an inspirational leader operating within a hospitality paradigm – is to make people feel good and happy about what they are doing. Hospitality is all about emotion and atmosphere! Staff that feel that they are being properly recognised for their efforts, will feel uplifted and far more inclined to expend discretionary effort; channelling positive emotions into their dealings with customers who – in turn – will feel warm, valued and cared for.

Outstanding ODs approach recognition in a genuine and authentic way; they don't create 'happy clappy' clubs. But how do the best ODs recognise their teams' performance?

- **'Leadership Style Fit'** – great ODs ensure that the way in which they recognise people mirrors their personality and style. For instance, extrovert ODs will make deposits in emotional bank accounts by publicly celebrating achievements and singing praises from the rooftops. They aren't virtue signalling; rather, this open, public approach is in keeping with their bubbly demeanour and personality. Other, introverted-type ODs will quietly put their arms around people, quietly recognising people who they have 'caught doing things right'. Each approach is, in its own particular way, a powerful show of gratitude because it doesn't look manu-factured; it comes from the heart.

- **'Tea Table Theory'** – also, outstanding ODs really understand the consequences that bestowing recognition has upon their people's feelings of identity and self-worth. I call it the 'Tea Table Theory'. When people come home from work and they are asked by their family how 'it went today', being able to say that the 'big boss handed me a certificate' or 'gave me extra time off or £100 for a meal' increases their sense of pride and self-esteem. Telling other people about their success raises their sense of rela-tive social standing, bolstering their feelings of well-being and security.

Also, outstanding ODs get the difference between what I call trans-actional and transformational recognition:

- **Transactional Recognition** – generally practised by poor ODs, transactional recognition is a forced, disingenuous process in which people are recognised on a 'tick the box' basis – for instance, holding 'winners' dinners' or award ceremonies because it is expected of them, rather than spontaneously wanting to do it. Poor ODs see recognition as a transactional 'rhythm and routine' of the business; something that they formally *have* to do. Preferring remoteness and detachment, they are inclined to dip into the business now and again, telling a few people 'you're amazing, you're amazing' before disappearing for six months!

- **Transformational Recognition** – ODs practising higher-order recognition create great feelings and memories amongst their field teams. They go beyond surface recognition, actively seeking to form *deep connections* with their people. For instance, this might involve hosting trips or two-day events where they deliber-ately spend quality time with their people, really getting to know them; allowing their people to peer into the human vulnerability that underlies their 'veneer of office'! This kind of transformational recognition creates longer-lasting outcomes (higher discretionary effort, productivity and loyalty) because it creates ties and bonds that will endure the test of time.

So, outstanding ODs practise recognition in authentic, idiosyncratic ways which reflect their style and personality, but their intended outcome is always the same: to acknowledge and reinforce the desirable behaviours that they want to see imitated throughout their region/brand. As an MD, I can visit certain regions/brands within my portfolio and 'see, feel and touch' the *cultural imprint* left by ODs that really motivate their teams by genuinely caring about, and recognising, excellent performance. On the flip side, I can also – during my time in the field – immediately pick up on ODs that don't 'leave anything of themselves' in the business. And funnily enough, the former are always more successful than the latter in terms of landing innovation, sustaining better financial results and breeding top talent!

## *VALUES-BASED LEADERSHIP*

The third thing that outstanding 'Leading to Win' ODs do is purposefully set the *cultural tone* of their region/brand by acting with *integrity* and consistently modelling the organisation's values in order to shape purposeful and intentional behaviours throughout their brand/region:

> In effect, my job is to build up the psychological contract… the challenge is how do I shape behaviours across 550 stores? … what they need to do is look at you and see how you behave – what matters to you… they've got to 'get you'… So what you've got to do is get out into the stores, modelling the values – spreading consistent messaging on 'doing the right things'… also backing it up with the comms that come out of your Monday-morning meetings (performance, fun, rewarding success) reinforcing the messages!
>
> Adrian Frid, National Operations Director, Caffè Nero

Modelling the values is a critical activity performed by ODs, because they are seen as the ultimate standard-bearers of morality and adjudicators of desired and permitted behaviour within their brands/regions. Their behaviour will be interpreted, copied and imitated, so it is vital that they:

- **Exert soft 'cultural control' (rather than just hard 'bureaucratic control') through:**
    - o *Agreeing* a permitted code of conduct with their tribe, underpinned by a strong set of values (e.g. 'trust one another', 'honest and straightforward', 'celebrate success', 'act maturely', 'look for solutions not problems', 'can-do atti- tude', 'help and look after one another', 'customer first', etc.)
    - o *Reinforcing* the code through visibility, stories, signalling and consistent messaging
    - o *Backing up* the code through even-handed and balanced decision-making.

In the end, outstanding ODs understand that their people crave boundaries and clarity on how they should behave and 'what good looks like'. As the 'Tribal Elder', the OD is the standard-bearer of the *cultural mores, customs and iconography* of their region/brand.

## CASE STUDY 7 – PRACTISING VALUE-BASED LEADERSHIP IN GROWING BRANDS

*Gavin Smith is the Managing Director for Pizza Pilgrims, a fast-growing artisan casual dining brand (13 sites, 330 employees). Previously, he was Operations Director for Wahaca, having graduated from BCU's MSc in Multi-Unit Leadership and Strategy Programme in 2013 (with distinction).*

To me – having worked for two values-based brands recently (Wahaca and Pizza Pilgrims) – values are an absolutely essential cultural corner- stone of young businesses. They give your organisation a rudder – a compass! They *bind people together culturally* with a common set of behaviours ('how we do things around here') and get people out of bed in the morning. Done right and *lived*, they make people happy. At Pizza Pilgrims, we see ourselves as having two superpowers: first, we are the experts and fanatics of Neapolitan pizza and, second, we have the happiest team. Underpinning these superpowers, our values define us and what we stand for. What are they?

We operate this business, focusing on three key drivers: guest, team and commercial. They are all interlinked. In terms of our values purposefully aligning the organisation around these three drivers, we have four:

- **Purposeful** – push yourself and focus relentlessly on *growing the business*. Create the best Neapolitan pizza, delight our guests and create happiness amongst our team!

- **Positive** – approach your work with *zest and enthusiasm*; display a can-do attitude – find solutions not problems!

- **Natural** – be yourself: display your *authentic personality* and embrace difference!

- **Inclusiveness** – *respect the views* and opinions of others; work with a 'one-team mentality'.

Coming from a large company background (where I had senior field positions), I must admit that I was initially sceptical about the power that relevant, meaningful values can have within organisations. Yes, large companies in this sector have values – but they seem pretty vacuous and meaningless when senior behaviours undermine them on a daily basis! The whole point is that they need to be owned, reinforced and brought alive by everyone in the organisation. Our founders and our people had a large role in shaping our values – so they own and believe in them. They are brought alive and reinforced *throughout our culture* by what we do, not just what we say. Some examples:

- **Purposeful** – in terms of sharpening up this value, we have added more focus upon 'growing the business'. How? By getting our business leaders to own their parts of the business and – in addition to creating great pizza, memorable customer experiences and happy teams – ensuring that our restaurants are clean, safe and legal at all times. Profit and standards aren't dirty words. They ensure our sustainability and reputation! Monthly business meetings that check that our actions are 'purposefully' growing the business underpin this value.

- **Positive** – we approach all business challenges with optimism and an expectation we can improve things. This especially holds true in turnaround situations. Take our Oxford store, for example. We were struggling to gain traction in the local market – the restaurant is located in a shopping centre and was failing to attract students. So, giving the GM time and resource, we came up with an idea: a 'create your own pizza competition'. Over 130 people attended (many students from the university) and the eventual winner – Sebastian – became a raving advocate of the brand, going viral on social media and YouTube, creating massive publicity for the restaurant and brand. We now have close links with social societies in 28 colleges; this restaurant is now massively successful. Why? Because we didn't give up on it!

- **Natural** – we encourage our teams and customers to be their natural selves – to express themselves. Take one of our GMs who loves his dogs. He held a 'Puppy Pilgrims' event on a Saturday at our Dean Street outlet, pulling in over 100 customers and their dogs. Also – for customers – we have embraced and encouraged 'pizza box art' amongst our customers. We display their creations on our website and in store; they give our brand additional inspiration and personality – also enabling us to link up with Arts Festivals.

- **Inclusive** – respecting the views of our people is crucial on key issues. Recently, we decided to change our pizzaiolo uniforms to update them and make them more distinctive. Consulting with our pizzaiolos (who practise a craft that has real status in Italy), they told us that they would like uniforms in four different colours, denoting levels of expertise. This notion of a Pizzaiolo Brigade, with real pride in their profession – reinforced by the symbolism of their uniforms – will also set us apart from the competition.

As we grow the brand over the next few years, some might say that the values we hold and enact every day will get sacrificed on the altar of bureaucratic scale. And this is an ever-present danger. As we grow, outsiders might come in and – advertently or inadvertently – *undermine or destroy our culture* by trashing our values: I've seen it happen before! But in doing so, they risk wrecking the DNA and soul of our business – one of the key reasons for our success. As long as I am here, that will not happen.

# #2 BUILDING CAPABILITY

Regarded as being symbiotic with Leading to Win, Building Capability was the competency rated second for outstanding OD practice by the twenty-seven respondents. The personal quality requirements for this competency include: high levels of aspiration, emotional intelligence, judgement and listening skills.

Quite simply, outstanding ODs build 'elite tribes' with strength and depth!

> Outstanding ODs that I've witnessed that have been supremely successful over a long period of time really inspired people to follow them and – just as importantly – they were brilliant at succession planning; creating a talent pipeline bursting with capability...
>
> Liz Phillips, ex-HRD, Krispy Kreme, Swissport, Macdonald Hotels, Orchid Pubs and Mitchells and Butlers

In many ways, it's such an obvious winning characteristic and attribute of great leaders, yet many 'also-ran' ODs fail to get its importance:

> Over the course of my UK and international career, I have witnessed some outrageously selfish and destructive behaviours by ODs. They don't promote talent, they hollow it out! How? By clearing out talent they regard as a threat... by claiming everyone else's successes as their own... driving people to the limit and leaving them as empty shells... not investing in training and development (which they see as an irretrievable sunk cost)... being more interested in their own advancement rather than taking satisfaction from the growth of their people.
>
> David Singleton, ex-Regional Vice President, Hard Rock Cafe

In competitive organisational circumstances – where the rewards from senior advancement are high – it is natural that some ODs believe that the best way to achieve their career goals is to climb up the ladder on the backs of others. However, this is a short-term strategy that will not stand the test of time. People work for *people* in multi-site hospitality! Units that are run by great GMs, with enthusiastic teams, can outperform local competitors by considerable margins! Losing or 'burning' great front-line leaders can cost the business dearly. So, what do the best do? Essentially, they *'strive for obsoletion'*[6] by building *learning cultures* with a formidable bench strength and they do so by practising three things, namely: *enticing and retaining* the best, *investing in high-performance development* and personally *stretching and coaching* their people to be the best they can be.

## ENTICES AND RETAINS TALENT

Outstanding ODs create cultures that many want to join but few want to leave. Indeed, the mark of a great OD is the extent to which many of their people actively wish to move with them or work with them again when they leave.

> Outstanding ODs co-opt the best people through a reputa-
> tion they have built up over time. People want to work in their
> team – either directly or indirectly – because they want to join
> a *progressive culture* that they know will improve and advance
> them. The stories that they have heard and the feeling they
> get about the culture tells them… 'this is going to be fun and
> I want to be part of a successful team'… Often, you will find
> that a retinue of talent will follow the best around the industry
> if and when they move on!
>
> Barrie Robinson, National Operations Director, Parkdean
> Resorts

Inevitably, the desire to join and stay in organisations will be mediated by other factors such as the 'employment brand' (reward, terms and conditions, fringe benefits, etc.). However, outstanding ODs can – in an industry with broadly comparable reward and benefit provision – gain competitive advantage in the war for talent by:

---

6   Great leaders essentially aim to reduce their 'indispensability' by creating empowered, elite teams that can (eventually) operate without them. By contrast, toxic leaders ramp up their indispensability by building an 'ark of mediocrity' around themselves for self-interested, protective reasons. For further reading on this concept, see Edger, C., and Heffernan, N., *Advanced Leader Coaching – Accelerating Personal, Interpersonal and Business Growth* (Oxford: Libri, 2020), pp. 52–5.

- **Having a Compelling Vision** – having an imaginative and uplifting vision that fuels the desire for people to join and stay.

- **Winning Brand/Format Proposition** – creating a 'winning mentality' based around a credible, sustainable, crave-able proposition that people want to be a part of.

- **Setting a High Bar** – ensuring that only people with the right attitude and service personality – who derive great pleasure in serving customers – are appointed to the right positions in the right places. This involves ruthlessly ensuring that new recruits 'fit' the 'elite team' ethos and culture, possessing the energy, passion and determination to succeed in a high-performance culture with clear career pathways and opportunities to progress.

- **Personal Involvement** – furthermore, 'grandfathering' the sign-offs of key recruitment and selection decisions (i.e. £1m+ site GMs and Lessees/Tenants who their businesses are entering into long commercial agreements with!) in order to regulate quality and create strong personal bonds.

- **Protecting People from Punishment** – by protecting good people who might have had a bad day (by overshooting labour, dropping stocks or having a bad environmental audit), giving them a second chance to shine rather than handing out summary or terminal punishments. This enables outstanding ODs to gain a reputation for empathy and fairness, increasing their levels of retention and followership.

### CASE STUDY 8 – STRENGTHENING THE PENINSULAR TRIBE

*Steve Worrall is the Managing Director of St Austell Pubs, Inns & Hotels (185 units – 150 tenanted, 35 managed – three Area Managers, three BDMs and five functional direct reports). Previously, Steve held senior field and marketing positions with S&N Retail, Spirit and Greene King.*

My life lesson as a senior field leader in hospitality is that it's all about the people! Building high-performance field tribes with their own identity, customs and sense of belonging unlocks powerful levels of commitment and discretionary effort. Since I've been at St Austell over the past three years, I've absolutely bought into this fact and consciously gone out of my way to *strengthen the culture of our family-owned business* by focusing upon raising the capability of our teams. Why? First, as a *peninsular trading business* in the South West, we have specific challenges relating to talent retention. Youngsters often leave Cornwall to seek career opportunities and progression in other parts of the UK – so it's vital that we *attract and develop* the best in St Austell so that they stay and grow with us! Second, as a medium-sized vertically integrated pub enterprise (with a distinctive brewing arm), as opposed to a big corporate, we need to develop people with *breadth*, who have the ability to work across a range of activities. Certainly, as MD, I have to lead the way on this, combining strategy with rolling my sleeves up to get things done at a local field level when needs must.

How have I gone about strengthening the St Austell retail tribe? Firstly, through leadership and alignment. Secondly, through raising the bar on commercial focus and professionalism.

- *Leadership and Alignment* – from the off, I've been quite specific with my team. Our *purpose* is to create a long-term, sustainable, family-owned business which will endure for future genera-tions. Our *mission* is to be a world-class hospitality business. All our *KPIs* and effort are clustered around three imperative objec-tives: TEAM (developing and strengthening our people so that they can deliver outstanding experiences for our guest), GUEST (providing the 'best of family' occasions that will make customers love us) and INVESTOR (grow sales and profit – in the right way – to delight our principal stakeholders). The way in which I have sought to embed all of these principles and aims is through casting my own 'positive shadow' over the business, constantly reinforcing the messages and recognising desired behaviours at all levels, at all times. Also, I believe in a 'high support/high chal-lenge' culture, in which people are trusted and feel safe to speak up without any fear of retribution. It is my job to listen, follow-up, coach and stretch people. The great thing about St Austell is that we can 'get our arms around' our people's development – because we are intimate and 'close', knowing the strengths and weaknesses of all our teams and tenants!

- *Commercial Focus and Professionalism* – inspiring people – giving them a sense of purpose and direction, combined with intensive development – is one arm of creating high-performing tribes. The other is instilling a sense of *commercial focus*, so that people can see and celebrate the financial benefits of professional execution. Although I generally apply a *light touch management model*, I have purposefully sharpened the saw in two specific areas. First, I've driven more efficient use of *capex* by planning, scheduling and landing new openings and refurbishments more effectively. The retail team now have more confidence – because they have seen the results! – that detailed, purposeful planning in this area (rather than a rushed, 'botched' approach) can substantially increase ROI on new projects within the first year. Second, I have helped educate the team to make better use of our *labour-scheduling* technology provided by S4 Labour. Our businesses are susceptible to huge variations in demand, due to seasonality, weather and tides; our capacity to forecast sales and plan labour rosters accordingly has a huge impact on the bottom line. Running 'fat' in non-peak or 'thin' in peak harms the business. In my first year, ramping up our skill level in this area and our improved use of capex saw sales grow by £1.2m and reduced labour by £250k, delivering a 15% increase in EBIT!

The effect of all of this has been to create a more cohesive, driven tribe. For sure, the success of the company in recent times has increased our people's feeling of pride in our unique family-owned company. The knock-on effects from this? Our retention rates have risen and the well-being of our people (a paramount aim in my eyes) remains strong. I have also taken great pleasure seeing so many of our people progressing; taking on bigger roles and challenges. Back in my 'big corporate' days, I saw too many ODs 'burning' good people by keeping them in situ because it served their own selfish agendas. At St Austell, it makes me immensely proud to see that we appreciate and fulfil the aspirations of people who want to grow and succeed with us in building an outstanding, sustainable peninsular business.

## *DEVELOPS A HIGH-PERFORMANCE TEAM*

Whilst constantly topping up the talent bank by recruiting and retaining quality people, outstanding ODs understand one elemental fact above all others (as Steve Worrall alludes to above): creating real bench strength within their regions/brands is derived from developing teams from within.

The reality is that, to create high-performing teams, you have to start with what you've got rather than importing in talent willy nilly from outside. A mistake poor ODs make – particularly naïve or 'green' appointments – is assuming that everyone they've inherited is crap. The best ones recognise that – besides topping up the capability with a couple of key appointments – the best way to create a high-performing team is by investing time, emotion and money in what you've got. Attitude + Aptitude = Altitude. Get their heads right, sharpen their skills and you will fly!

John Dyson, National Operations Director, Mecca Bingo

Outstanding ODs develop high-performing teams[7] in two ways, by:

- **Optimising Team Performance**
  - o **Team Lifecycle** – diligently taking their direct AM/BDM team through the 'forming, storming, norming, performing and adjourning' cycle to ensure optimal performance.

    (Outstanding ODs will be mindful of the fact that their optimum team/portfolio 'impact lifespan' is probably about five years!)

  - o **Continuity** – preserving regional/brand continuity among Areas and Clusters so that trust, capability and momentum can be built up. (Too many ODs fiddle with Area and Cluster leadership and boundaries, disrupting important bonds and relationships that keep the show on the road.)

  - o **Freshening Up** – but (counterintuitively) also calling the optimum time for GMs and AM/BDMs in specific units/areas. Often, GMs peak at the end of their second year in post; AMs in their third year. Outstanding ODs are skilled at rotating talent around the portfolio, keeping people fresh by *deftly* presenting them with new challenges at the right time.

- **Developing Team Skills**
  - o **Technical** – investing in important skills such as health and

---

7   For wider reading on leadership and high-performance teams, see 'Coaching Leaders to Develop Teams' in Edger, C., and Heffernan, N., *Advanced Leader Coaching – Accelerating Personal, Interpersonal and Business Growth* (Oxford: Libri, 2020), pp. 141–53.

safety, food production/service, service-cycle execution and administration (labour scheduling, payroll, BOH procedures, etc.).

o **Behavioural** – bolstering area, unit and shift leadership and service-cycle capabilities in order to optimise the customer experience.

o **Cognitive** – sharpening problem-solving, project-management and decision-making skills so that initiatives can be landed on time, to specification; getting people to think for themselves rather than always being told what to do.

o **Progression Paths** – having clearly signposted development and progression routes for aspiring employees to 'mindmap' the opportunity, at least, of *meritocratic* 'bar to boardroom' progression.

---

## CASE STUDY 9 – DEVELOPING A HIGH-PERFORMANCE TRIBE

*Vanessa Hall, the Non-Executive Chair of Cubitt, was previously the Chair and CEO of Vapiano S.E. (230 managed and franchised units worldwide), the CEO of YO! Sushi (75 units in the UK and US) and Divisional MD of Mitchells and Butlers (circa 200 units – five brands: Premium Country Dining Group, Village Pub and Kitchen, Miller and Carter, All Bar One and Browns).*

Strong tribes require a strong identity, purpose and set of common values, so the starting point for ODs trying to build successful regional/brand teams is to lay out a compelling vision that attracts and retains like-minded people who share similar aspirations and beliefs. That is *not to say that outstanding ODs try to clone everyone or create an unquestioning cult*; rather, they are intent upon gathering an elite tribe of individuals that *trust* one another in pursuance of a meaningful, shared noble cause. This sense of trust is also enhanced by ODs that set out their *clear expectations* (in terms of behaviours, standards and delivery) because people like boundaries and are keen to understand (and perform to) 'what good looks like'. In short – to reiterate – outstanding ODs who develop high-performing teams define a clear, uplifting direction, underpinned by strong values that shape their teams' behaviours, accelerating them on a journey to the desired destination.

Having provided the setup, how do they lead and develop these high-performing regional/brand teams? First, leadership. Outstanding ODs are optimistic and proactive. Why? Being continuously 'on show' in meetings and in the field, they need to maintain an aura of infectious, positive energy which motivates and galvanises their team. They also create symbols, icons and stories that instil a vibrant tribal identity – *celebrating* legendary achievements, landmarks and successes. Why? Emotionally contagious leadership has far greater resonance than dry, logical managerialism!

Second, development. Outstanding ODs aren't just 'compass setters' and great cheerleaders; they also train, develop, nurture and grow superb talent and skills – driving a *meritocratic culture* – across their portfolio *at all levels*, in three respects:

- **Technical Competence** – many of the premium fresh-led brands I have led at a senior level have required a high degree of technical execution. This has meant that operators at all levels have required intensive induction and remedial training on fresh ingredient preparation, cooking and delivery. Obviously, all brands have had strong blueprint specifications, sufficient field training support and in-depth auditing/correction procedures. But the best means by which outstanding ODs inject technical excellence into their regions/brands is – in my experience – through instilling an immense sense of *cultural pride* around their *craftsmanship* of the product. People will deliver a quality product – to the desired specification – not because it's about ticking a compliance box; rather, they *care* passionately about producing the highest-quality dishes and/or operating the safest hospitality environments (especially post-COVID). Their sense of pride is injured if it isn't done right!

- **Behavioural Competence** – at AM level, I have found that leadership and service training and development are best done as an *inclusive* activity. That is to say, the whole senior region/brand team does development from the same provider (say Covey or Coverdale) at the same time, to ensure everyone goes at the same speed and achieves the same amount of buy-in and understanding. Often, behavioural ('soft skills') training will involve 'train the trainer' aspects, where each level sequentially trains the next level down. After all, to teach it is to master it! One issue, however, that confronts all ODs at present – with regards to service behaviour – is generational. ODs need to work hard to attract a new generation into this industry and then ensure that these millennials learn the importance of interactive guest care and hospitality service. We are a people business not a tech business!

- **Cognitive Competence** – in addition to training and developing people to deliver a quality product and service experience, outstanding ODs need to develop the critical thinking capabilities of their people. Why? Hospitality can be defined in terms of precise product assembly, defined service steps and so forth, but the truth is that it comprises a thousand moving parts (especially in premium environments). Also, businesses are never in a steady-state position – they are (at various junctures) either growing or shrinking. Therefore – at all levels of their region/brand – ODs need to get people to think independently about how they solve problems in an agile, responsive manner in order to rectify missteps. How? I have always found that outstanding ODs achieve this through *delegation and trust*. People learn through doing it themselves and (often) making mistakes. Levels of resilience and critical thinking flow from empowerment rather than close control!

In addition to establishing a vision, creating a positive climate and focussing upon technical, behavioural and cognitive development, outstanding ODs also 'unlock' and create *clear promotional pathways* for their people, creating a clear sense of 'achievable aspiration'. Also, they keep a close eye on up-and-coming talent by actively supporting it through *customised development interventions*. As an Operations Director myself twenty years ago, I was actively involved in the development of a high-potential trainee in my business. I am proud to say that this person now features as a case-study contributor elsewhere in this book!

# *CHALLENGES AND STRETCHES PEOPLE*

The third major element of Building Capability for outstanding ODs is often missed by generic leadership books that emphasise the merits of 'soft HR', namely challenging and stretching their people. Outstanding ODs aren't soft touches – they have *clear expectations*, confronting and addressing performance issues. But instead of jumping on people, they have direct, honest conversations designed to nip problems in the bud or get the best out of people:

> Bad ODs will keep their distance with their people – deliberately – and just rule by fear; jumping on them during appraisals or by acting in a passive-aggressive manner. The best ones? Whilst they maintain a professional distance, *they are clear about what they expect*, actively challenging and stretching their people through having frank, honest conversations. This might be through coaching, mentoring or just one-to-one chats; but it is done with the best of intentions. They raise the self-awareness and capability of their people by getting them to acknowledge *what* and *why* they need to improve. Most importantly, they then provide them with the tools that give them the means *how* to improve!
>
> Karen Forrester, ex-CEO, TGI Fridays

Interestingly, this trait is usually more common in female ODs – explaining why (according to the twenty-seven research respondents) they usually outperform their male counterparts! By having tough conversations with their people, they get to the heart of issues, addressing the root causes rather than the symptoms. What are the techniques that outstanding ODs use? One or other of the following approaches:

- **Courageous Coaching** – patiently listening and asking *tough*, probing questions; ensuring that that their people come up with the solutions themselves (which decreases dependency)[8].

- **Wise Mentoring** – passing on learnt experiences on how to resolve particular dilemmas or problems.

---

8  For further reading on Courageous Coaching, see Edger, C., *Courageous Coaching using the BUILD–Raise Method* (Oxford: Libri, 2017).

- **Honest and Direct Feedback** – giving balanced, specific, non-judgemental, honest feedback that helps recipients (who are on 'receive') really advance.

*CASE STUDY 10 – STRETCHING PEOPLE TO BE THE BEST VERSIONS OF THEMSELVES!*

*David Singleton has spent over 30 years in the hospitality and retail industry in the USA, EMEA and South Asia as a brand builder, creator, operator, franchisee and franchisor for some of the world's best-known and respected brands. Before he left the corporate world for wider consulting and executive coaching, he was the Regional Vice President for Hard Rock Cafe, responsible for franchising and business development in EMEA and South Asia.*

Outstanding ODs are very giving with their time, taking on coaching and mentoring responsibilities for people that either sit outside their brand/region or who are not direct reports. Why is this important? Because coaching and mentoring conversations provide a *safe place* for coachees and mentees to discuss issues that they wouldn't normally discuss with their bosses. Also – done well – it develops the *self-awareness* of coachees/mentees, brings out their *latent inner knowledge* and helps them develop strong *networks and relationships* around the organisation. In particular, I believe coaching and mentoring really help with *talent planning and succession processes*. Great coaching/mentoring ODs who have been through the journey can help their coachees/mentees understand the pitfalls and opportunities that might lie before them – helping them to navigate smoother career-progression paths. It is particularly important in international organisations where these paths can seem rather opaque and poorly signalled.

In relation to what outstanding ODs do with their direct teams – complementing the application of some 'light' forms of coaching and mentoring – I have found that they are all good at one thing: *honest, direct, challenging feedback* that really stretches people. And they do it with the best of intentions – they really do want their people to be the best versions of themselves. How do they do it? In (subtly) *soft* and *hard* ways:

- **Humble Inquiry** – hard conversations are always difficult to have – most people shy away from holding them or avoid them. Rather than saying 'What the hell is going on here George? Explain yourself!', one way of having a direct conversation without seeming confrontational is to ask the simple questions: *'could you take me through what you are doing here?'* or *'tell me what you see – explain to me what you think the issues are.'* This way, you have taken a positive approach, removing any personal judgement by asking people to reflect upon their own actions/behaviours… getting them to come up with the observations and (possibly) solutions that you would have made yourself! Because operators are insanely overloaded, often they can't see the wood from the trees; but if you get them to *stop, observe and think*, they will almost always get to the answer themselves.

- **Direct Feedback** – but sometimes – depending on context, circumstances and personalities – a more direct approach is required. ODs are busy people and sometimes they don't have the time to mess around. They need to jolt people – *taking them out of their comfort zone in order to stretch them*. In these instances, saying *'you have disappointed me because I thought better of you – now show me what you can do!'* is a more appropriate approach. But by signalling their respect for the individual ('I thought better of you'), they are always leaving the recipient with the belief that their OD is fundamentally on their side.

Where have I seen feedback done well or badly?

- **Industrial Myopia** – talking personally, I once worked in a senior field position for an international brand that worked in extreme silos and had operators that had been in situ for decades. My senior field peers had a 'tick box' compliance mentality where they conducted 'royal' field visits, checking noticeboards, daily work sheets and audit manuals. What they didn't do was have the *curiosity to ask questions, listen and respect the contributions of others*. I called this 'industrial myopia' because, if they had taken more of a people-centric approach, they would have got far more out of the business! The lack of coaching, mentoring and humble enquiry 'culture' in that business really prevented it – in my view – from being truly world class.

- **Servant Leadership** – but then I have worked in businesses whose values and mode of operating are far closer to my paradigm. I remember being given the book *Servant Leadership* by one of my bosses nearly 20 years ago – it was a game changer for me. This notion that in order to receive optimal performance you 'give something of yourself to others'. And I can remember as an OD really pushing some of my people – who have subsequently gone on to great things – really hard; not because I wanted to destroy them but because I knew that they could be so much better. I spent so much time with them; challenging them, getting them to solve their own problems – to be the best versions of themselves. Although they didn't like it at the time – they tell me now that they know I did it for *them* not myself!

So, in summary I would say that being able to coach, mentor and give great feedback is a form of *real competitive advantage* for outstanding ODs. Why? The only cost is *time, effort and emotional investment* – but the payback (in terms of seeing people and the business progress) is huge! I've worked across 40 countries and seven time zones in my career and *I can only be me* – not anyone else. My technique has never differed. *Care* about and give your time and attention to others – through coaching, mentoring and quality feedback – and you stretch people to achieve extraordinary results.

# #3 INFLUENCING AND ALLIANCE BUILDING

The competency ranked third for outstanding ODs is Influencing and Alliance Building. This is where outstanding ODs develop the capability to leverage internal functional resources (that don't typically report directly into them) by creating harmonious reciprocal relationships which result in win–win outcomes. In order to do so, they need to exhibit exceptional personal maturity, diplomacy, emotional control and social intelligence[9]!

In actual fact, this is one of the competencies upon which, in their early days, most ODs fall short! Coming from the AM position where (perhaps) their

---

9    For wider reading on stakeholder influencing and management, see 'Coaching Leaders to Align Stakeholders' in Edger, C., and Heffernan, N., *Advanced Leader Coaching – Accelerating Personal, Interpersonal and Business Growth* (Oxford: Libri, 2020), pp. 153–65.

default position was to blame and castigate support functions, they carry this attitude and behaviour through to a more senior level:

> ODs that come up from AM positions often take their silo mentality with them in which they consciously or unconsciously label all people at the centre as idiots – frequently losing their temper over Head Office breakdowns and cock ups! This immature attitude, however, is ultimately self-harming; great ODs get wise to the fact that the easiest way to get things done is to make alliances and not be pig-headed!
>
> Martin Nelson, Operations Director, Premium Country Pubs
> (Mitchells and Butlers)

The actual reason why many AMs have generally adopted an anti-centre attitude in the first place is understandable. Detached from operations, functional personnel rarely work at their speed and – invariably – have other priorities to deal with. But at OD level, operators become exposed to Functional Heads and – if they are sensible enough – they start to (as Covey exhorts) empathise and 'understand the other person's world':

> The reality is that central stakeholders have enormous pressures and targets too. You achieve more by understanding what their objectives are and helping them to achieve them. Through this, you will create essential alliances. Bullying won't work with HR, Property, Finance, Marketing etc. ... it just makes them shut up shop for you!
>
> Adam Fowle, ex-Senior Non-Executive Director, Ei Group

Clearly, extending the hand of friendship and displaying an understanding mentality with the centre will benefit ODs and their regions/brands in the long run. They will find that they jump the queue for resolving operational problems (*reducing levels of unnecessary interference*) and new product/initiative launches. But the best ODs are also adept – whilst helping and reciprocating with Head Office – at preserving some degree of local customisation and agility; something that Functional Heads are willing to turn a blind eye to if their broader agendas are being achieved! Thus, the three main practices mastered by outstanding ODs – *build central reciprocation, jointly solve systemic problems and integrate the region/brand* – will now be considered in turn.

## *BUILDS CENTRAL RECIPROCATION*

Outstanding ODs get the fact that in today's hyper-connected hospitality organisations – which are becoming more reliant on complex digital and technological solutions to capture sales and contain costs – they have to manage their inter-dependencies at Head Office:

> Back in the day, kick-arse ODs regarded themselves as gods – the holders of the P&L. They were the rainmakers! They alone produced the profit for the company! They expected all and sundry to bow to them and if they told the functions to jump, they expected to be asked 'how high?' This is no longer a viable way of operating. The impact and influence the central functions have on their bottom line – be it through digital sales/marketing, property investments, product innovation, format repositioning or labour scheduling systems – means that they have to reciprocate and work together with the functional experts to achieve the best outcomes. Staying in your trench and lobbing hand grenades at the centre is not a viable strategy for twenty-first-century ODs. I for one will not accept that behaviour!
>
> Simon Longbottom, CEO, Stonegate Group

Accepting the fact that outstanding ODs build strong ties and bonds with central functions which lead to reciprocating behaviours, how do they achieve this in practice?

- **Respect** – rather than disparaging central personnel in humiliating terms, they actively demonstrate (in front of their teams) that they respect their expert opinion. This ensures that not only do people from the centre feel more valued and disposed to help but also, the OD's team imitates their collaborative behaviour – making life far easier at the centre.

- **Resources/Interest Overlap** – in addition, outstanding ODs either consciously or unconsciously map who can be the greatest help to them in growing sales and *reducing interference* by identifying those that have the most resources (expertise, ideas, money, etc.) combined with the greatest vested interest in their success.

- **Uncover Hidden Value** – having understood the objectives of the prime functional 'helpers', great ODs deftly 'make their agenda the central agenda' by helping to 'uncover hidden value' that will help both parties mutually achieve their respective goals!

## CASE STUDY 11 – CREATING WIN–WIN SOLUTIONS WITH CENTRAL FUNCTIONS

*Liz Phillips has operated at a senior level within the hospitality industry for over 30 years, holding HR Director positions in Mitchells and Butlers, Orchid Pubs, MacDonald Hotels, Krispy Kreme and Swissport. In 2011, she was named in the Hospitality Women Power 100 and has won several awards in the past from NITA, Springboard, CBI, Personnel Today, etc.*

ODs must have the capability to influence stakeholders (particularly at the centre). *Why?* Because, *firstly*, functional leaders are experts within their particular domain. You wouldn't go to a doctor and diagnose your own illness. If ODs don't think that the functional expert understands what their issue and requirement is, instead of flouncing off saying that 'they're all useless', (s)he needs to have a mature dialogue where (s)he makes their case. After all, functional staff have a load of pressing priorities too. *Secondly*, working with central functions is important because multi-unit leisure companies can only gain the benefits of economies of scale (consistency, replication, standardisation, efficiency, process and systems alignment) if ODs are willing to build a *collaborative culture* with the centre – particularly during restructures where sharing resources may be required. ODs that think that they can negotiate everything and plead a special case in every circumstance – thereby defeating the object of 'optimal chain-scale efficiencies' – are (potentially) robbing their organisation of considerable value.

How do the best ODs get central functional leaders onside? The best ones come to you with a dilemma combined with:

- A clarity of vision about where they want to get to

- A real willingness to build strong relationships with those who can help them

- A proper commercial underpinning of their idea/solution/initiative

- A straightforward approach to getting things done.

Central functional leaders are far more likely to respect and buy into ODs that adopt this approach. In fact, in my experience, you can see ODs that operate like this gaining traction simultaneously across all functional heads – co-opting resources (time, effort and money) to back their value-added initiatives. They work hard at getting everyone aligned to their vision! But the main point is this: what they are selling is usually of *strategic* rather than *tactical* value. Rather than being trivial, what the OD is drawing the central function in on has a manifest strategic commercial impact – something that most functional heads worth their salt will definitely be willing to devote their time and resources to make happen.

Let me give you two real-life examples of ODs that worked with central functions to create real win–win outcomes. Both were proactive, energetic and dynamic 'turnaround MDs':

- **'Carvery Turnaround OD'** – the first OD that comes to mind had been recruited externally by us from a company that had gone bust – I was on the interview panel. He impressed us at interview, so we appointed him into an asset that had been failing for some time; a low-margin carvery business with about 70 units. This could have turned out to be a hospital pass, but he turned it into a launchpad for his career with us (eventually ending up as a Divisional MD). On joining, he immediately galvanised his troops and reached out to central functional leaders for assistance. It was clear he wanted to make a name for himself. At the same time, we had just bought an asset of over 100 units that contained some pubs with pizza ovens and 'pizza parlour' areas; they were incredibly successful (low margin/high volume). This OD was extremely investigative and curious; always keen to see and learn new ways of doing things. The integration team for the acquisition reached out to him and he did likewise. Why not combine his carveries with an integrated pizza offering? Working through the functional teams, this OD created great relationships to make things happen fast: in pretty quick order, 30 carvery units were converted into the dual offer. The result? It provided a major margin and sales spike in his brand that reversed its previous decline, also leading to a new brand format being rolled out across the company!

- *'London Turnaround OD'* – this OD led a multi-brand portfolio with a problem. Its units in London were performing poorly in relation to both the competition and the rest of the company. Why? Staff turnover was high, sales were anaemic, customer feedback was patchy and standards were variable across the brands. What did she do? She set up a London Taskforce that comprised all of the functions to a) sharpen up the brand propositions, b) set some aspirational commercial targets and c) resolve some of the operational and employee engagement issues. Cross-functional meetings for each format were held in conjunction with the Operations Team in order to raise the bar in all of the brands and formats across the London region. In my case, I was tasked to capture and analyse employee feedback data to understand why turnover was so high in some formats. This might seem obvious now, but back then – in this organisation – employee feedback mechanisms weren't standard across the company. I got a whiz kid graduate to put the survey together and implement it quickly. The result? We found out pretty quickly that there was a connection between controlling and autocratic leadership styles, poor rates of employee satisfaction, high levels of turnover, low customer satisfaction and declining sales. The OD acted upon this information immediately, creating a high degree of peer pressure amongst her field leaders to sort this out! Which they did – and to great effect. Over the next two years, the London region smashed its budget in a complete turnaround of fortunes plotted by the OD with help from the functions.

So, in summary, I would say that the outstanding ODs I have dealt with over my career have definitely mastered the art of deftly influencing central functions – particularly in large organisations where the agendas of functional leaders might lie in other areas. On the other hand, those ODs that 'don't let anyone else in', are too controlling, fail to give straight answers and indulge in excessive gameplay with functional experts will – in the end – be hoisted by their own petard. Because when they really need help, their past behavioural record will count against them and they will be left friendless and isolated from valuable central resources.

## *FLAGS SYSTEMIC ISSUES*

Having built up a high level of reciprocation, there will be times when the OD urgently needs to call down favours from Head Office:

> Things never run smoothly in multi-site leisure operations! There are too many moving parts. That is why this job – if you let it – can consume you 24/7; the issues and problems you encounter are never ending. What you have to do is discriminate between really systemic problems (deep-rooted showstoppers) that are seriously derailing your whole operation and the minor irritants that people are moaning about but aren't really the 'big bugs'. In franchise, franchisees will often highlight every little thing as being a significant problem. I can't overburden the centre will all of this – I have to fix the showstoppers with them rather than the tiddlers!
>
> Elton Gray, Commercial and Operations Manager, Creams Café

Obviously, one of the main roles of the OD is to act as a senior intermediary between the centre and the line. But in order to ensure field operations run smoothly – removing unnecessary bottlenecks and 'pain points' – they must interpret, synthesise and articulate what the main systemic problems are by:

- **Gathering Intelligence** – great ODs keep closely in touch with front-line operations – talking with their trusted senior AMs and 'big dog' GMs – to monitor and watch out for any systemic malfunctions.

- **Filtering the Facts** – but they have to apply a filter to what they are told by their AMs and GMs. Who's raising minor issues just to play games or settle functional scores? Where do underperformance issues really lie – in negative field-based behaviours *or* central planning, process or systems errors?

- **Engaging the Centre** – having established where the showstoppers or interference might lie, outstanding ODs diplomatically engage 'friends' in central functions either formally (politely in meetings or in writing) or informally (over the phone, in the corridor or via MTeams) to gain urgent assistance in resolving the issues.

## CASE STUDY 12 – RESOLVING SYSTEMIC ISSUES WITH THE CENTRE

*Mike O'Connor is an Operations Director with Greene King Pub Partners responsible for circa 300 leased and tenanted businesses, with eight BDM direct reports. A field-operations veteran, Mike graduated from BCU's MSc in Multi-Unit and Strategy Programme in 2013 (with distinction).*

If you look at multi-unit hospitality organisations as bowties, the ODs sit in the middle: between the field and the centre. In this sense, the OD is in a unique position, metaphorically using their right hand for strategizing and dealing with the centre, whilst deploying their left hand for articulation and implementation in the field. But they also fulfil another vital function. As our primary aim is to execute the strategy of the company and optimise the performance of our regions, it is crucial that we remove any impediments or obstacles for our team. Why? Misguided processes, policies and initiatives can slow us down; I need to understand from my BDMs what the company needs to 'stop, start or continue' to ensure they optimise our partnerships with our tenants. If things are getting in our way, I can (judiciously) use my clout to sort out bottlenecks and rate limiters quickly.

But how do I go about cutting down on bureaucracy and changing central processes that hamper our delivery?

- ***Filter the 'Noise'*** – the first thing to say is that, on any given day, ODs will get moans from their BDMs that they can't do 'x, y or z' because the 'centre is getting in the way'. My job is to filter this feedback, looking to see if the complaints form a broader pattern around certain issues. Are there more related examples? What is the *actual* commercial effect of their 'cited' impediments? To this end, you really need to know and trust your team. ODs (especially new ones who haven't done the role) can get played by BDMs who use the centre as a distraction for their own poor performance. Charging into the functions and raising hell over an issue that is a random event or inconsequential breakdown will destroy your credibility and influence! You have to do your groundwork – is this just a 'political whine' or is what is being raised (by 'serious' BDMs) part of a theme? You can't keep crying wolf – I have to have real evidence that something is genuinely destroying value for my team and their pub partners.

- **Pick your Moment** – if you've established that there is a genuine system or process malfunction that is costing your region time and money, you still can't rush in to get things fixed immediately. You've got to pick the right moment and relevant decision-making forum for maximum effect. Is it a credit control, marketing support, licensee recruitment or property maintenance/investment issue? When are the meetings that relate to your systemic issue being held? Who will be attending the meeting? What decisions need to be made to rectify the situation?

- **Lobby Key Decision-Makers** – having established the forum in which you can sort out a 'blocker' that's costing you money, you've got to get the key decision-makers onside beforehand. Starting with your peers (the other ODs), you might build a coalition going into the meeting, adding strength and validity to your cause. If it is a really emotive issue, you also really need to pre-warn or inform the functional heads that you are going to *diplomatically* raise an issue, so that they aren't blindsided or embarrassed. Good ODs will already have built mature relationships in the centre, and this is a time when they need to draw down upon the goodwill and 'credit'. Also, good ODs will have built a compelling case that what is hampering them (from a central control point of view) is unequivocally derailing the organisation's strategy – something that most functional heads would not wish to be seen doing, anyway!

Outstanding ODs know the *culture and politics* of an organisation. They know who the opinion-formers are and what they have to do to get them onside. Let me give you a couple of examples (one good, one bad) where I have seen ODs get this right or wrong.

- **Futile 'Charging In'** – over the thirty-odd years I've been in the field, I've observed the behaviours of ODs who've been brought in from outside or have landed with us as a result of an acquisition. Almost without exception, they have come unstuck pretty quickly. Why? In one instance, we acquired a company and the senior field leaders who transitioned over didn't make any effort to assimilate into our culture. Their attitude was 'your processes are slow and archaic', 'your systems are out of date' and 'your rules and procedures are too tight'. This was in spite of us having out-performed the market over the previous seven years! They might have been right to some degree; but their behaviour in meetings and around the business was toxic. They generated a high degree of tension and friction, constantly banging the table. In the end, they got nowhere and eventually departed the business.

- *Sophisticated Influencing* – recently we had an issue in the business; we had a fair amount of capex at our disposal and some brilliant pub partners with some great schemes that would really add joint value. Our BDMs were chomping at the bit and we wanted to accelerate our profit performance. The question was, therefore, how can we accelerate the capex programme? The issue was that the investment thresholds and sign-off procedures were too low and too slow, respectively. So what I and my colleagues did was lobby our Finance and Property Heads – 'can we increase the thresholds and speed up the decision-making process? If we do, we can make the company more money, faster! It fits with our strategic aspiration to optimise our assets more fully, rebalancing the value–premium mix of our portfolio!' These were mature, behind-the-scenes conversations and resulted in a new, slicker procedure being signed off. Suddenly we were able access capex quicker and break ground speedily – giving us and our partners an extra four months of benefit within the financial year!

So, the reality is this: listen, watch and filter. Assimilate and pick the big rocks. Locate and influence the decision-makers in a persuasive, rather than confrontational, manner. The outcome? You can really help drive the business on with a team that is fired up by the fact that you are making their job easier to win, rather being demotivated by you standing back – doing nothing – or firing blanks!

## INTEGRATES BRAND/REGION

In addition to reciprocating and resolving systemic problems – demonstrating higher-order Influencing and Alliance Building capabilities – outstanding ODs are (as alluded to above) judicious about ensuring that their region/brand walks the fine line between total central conformance and declaring local UDI:

The best ODs are clever in the way they integrate their regions/brands into the corporate body without totally submitting to its tyranny. Indeed, they are sensitive to the fact that unless their people feel that they demonstrate sufficient pushback or influence, they will be perceived as weak… merely an apologist for the centre. So they must be seen to be securing some big wins through their influencing and alliances to shape important policy matters!

Clive Chesser, CEO, Punch Pubs & Co

To this extent, outstanding ODs take a holistic view of both their organisations and businesses. There will be some occasions when some tough asks are imposed by the centre (in terms of labour costs, compliance and standardisation) but the OD decides to lose a few battles to win the war. They cannot ever propagate an all-out 'insider versus outsider' (them and us) struggle because they know that such a strategy will result in zero-sum gains. Policy and strategic gains (see 'Strategic Thinking' below) will be more likely to be gained through:

- **Alignment** – to organisational non-negotiables (with appropriate tailoring and 'workarounds' that will help meet the 'ends' if not the 'means'!)
- **Inclusivity** – including functional personnel in regional/brand decision-making; making them feel welcome at meetings and publicly recognising their efforts.
- **Negotiation** – making strong business cases for any *major* deviations/changes to initiatives or policies.
- **Navigation** – deftly navigating the requirement for central alignment versus the visceral need for local autonomy and self-expression!

## CASE STUDY 13 – WORKING IN PARTNERSHIP WITH THE CENTRE

*Keith Palmer is the National Town Centre Operations Manager for Marston's (four AMs and 55 units). Previously, he held AM positions in managed, L&T and franchised formats. In 2016, he graduated from the Multi-Unit Leadership and Strategy MSc Programme at BCU with distinction.*

Area Managers will often think and believe 'it's my area and I know best!' They have a tendency to dismiss or undervalue the contribution of central functional personnel. It is connected to the fact that AMs perceive themselves as 'keepers of the P&L' (in contrast to the 'desk jockeys' at the centre), the 24/7 intensity of their role (as opposed to Head Office nine-to-fivers!) and their belief – because they execute a multitude of property, HR, finance and marketing-related tasks – that they 'know' and can do *any* job better than HQ. In short, too many AMs perceive the centre as being the problem not the solution. Prior to becoming an OM, I was probably guilty of some of these attitudes and behaviours myself. Also, when I was promoted to OM, I carried some this baggage into my new role and found myself (briefly) at loggerheads with some functional personnel.

However, what I found out quite quickly was that – in reality – most people in the centre are only trying to help. Also, they are the experts. If you build relationships with them, they can provide you with the extra tools and solutions you need to improve your portfolio performance. But, how do you build really strong relationships with Head Office experts to gain real commercial traction? I'll give you three examples where pursuing a collaborative approach has yielded results for me.

- **Designing the Proposition** – when I took over the Town Centre portfolio five years ago, I was given a fairly wide brief; it was a new role, with a blank canvas. At first, *Marketing* had a strong view on how we should position our formats across the board based on 'battleship site' successes in major conurbations. However, I was able to bring my operational experience to bear by *educating, challenging and pushing back*; getting the marketers to closely analyse customer analytics in secondary and medium-sized towns. In the end, the product we *jointly engineered* had a greater in-built local flexibility, enabling us to be more agile in selective micro-markets. This approach has served us well, with the Town Centre portfolio exceeding our expectations over the past few years; but ultimately, it was a *joint enterprise* – marketing expertise allied to operational nous!

- **Safeguarding the Assets** – anyone who has run Town Centre units recognises that a 'safety and security first' approach is essential. When I assumed the position, door security costs were lumped into the variable labour cost line, assuming that we could flex costs in response to traffic and demand. But the fact is this: most Town Centre sites have door staff conditions attached to their licences – this is a non-negotiable element of legally running the premises! What I did here was go to *Finance* and *make a case* for moving door costs into the fixed costs line to unequivocally ensure that we abided by our legal and moral obligations. To a certain extent, it changed some of the P&L ratios but it was the right thing to do – taking the pressure off the GMs and safe-guarding our assets.

- **Reviving Closed Sites** – it is a fallacy to think that HQ is there to stop you from unlocking sales or profit. Over the past couple of years, I have further strengthened my bonds with the centre by working jointly with *Property* to revive closed Town Centre assets that were still costing us rental monies. I did this by requesting a list of closed units, selecting a few that I thought could be regen-erated and then working on a couple of 'revivals' *in partnership* with Property and Estates. The results have been extremely posi-tive, enabling the company to benefit by pulling 'write-off' rental payments back into the P&L and sourcing additional (previously unbudgeted) income streams.

In my view, you can build the centre's trust and confidence in you if you work with them rather than against them. Also, it helps if you acknowledge their contribution! Every month, in addition to recognising the Operator and Team Member of the Month, my team and I formally award a bottle of fizz and signed card (from all of the team) to the central person who we perceive has been the biggest help to us over the past month. We also spend a lot of time out in trade with central personnel to build relationships and show them (without gilding the lily) how full on it is out on the front-line of operations. In addition, I always invite key people from the centre to my monthly meetings – not as bystanders, but to discuss new initia-tives, improvements and products that will really drive the business forward. Co-operating, rather than competing with or disrespecting the centre, is in my view an essential ingredient of success for outstanding ODs.

# #4 STRATEGIC THINKING

The competency ranked fourth in order of importance for outstanding OD performance is Strategic Thinking. This is an OD's ability to set a clear direction for their region/brand, backed up with sufficient resources that will deliver competitive advantage over the medium to long term. The personal requirements for this include higher-order analytical capability, cognitive thinking capacity, imagination and problem-solving skills[10].

It is problematic for many AMs transitioning into the role for a number of reasons:

> AMs – even high-performing AMs of long standing – often struggle with this competency at OD level. Why? First, they have been used to planning and looking ahead by weeks or months rather than one- or three-year horizons. Second, their performance has been derived through motivating and engaging people – their strategic thinking has been done elsewhere by someone else! Third, they lack the intellectual horsepower to investigate, assimilate and draw insights from a lot of data... and they are shocking at writing incisive, Board-level reports! Accordingly, this is why some of the best AMs never make it at OD level.
>
> Steve Worrall, Managing Director, St Austell Pubs, Inns & Hotels

By contrast, outstanding ODs:

> Get the bigger picture. They have the ability to look beyond just the month and the short-term horizon (like AMs). They look to build businesses over a one-, three- or five-year term to ensure success and set us up for competitive advantage. Day to day, ensuring we have the cleanest restaurants and fulfil our 190-second service standard is crucial – but it is still just a process! To get us to the next level, they have to think strategically...
>
> Doug Wright, CEO, Wright Restaurants T/A McDonald's Restaurants

---

10  For wider reading on strategy and leadership, see 'Coaching Leaders to Clarify Strategy' in Edger, C., and Heffernan, N., *Advanced Leader Coaching – Accelerating Personal, Interpersonal and Business Growth* (Oxford: Libri, 2020), pp. 166–77.

Obviously, in smaller multi-site hospitality enterprises where the OD might typically sit on the Executive Board, a larger strategic input will be required on a more frequent basis. By contrast, in large multi-format corporates, where ODs report into Divisional MDs, their strategic input might be thought – in theory at least – to be a lesser priority. However, this is a fallacy! The clue is in the job title: ODs are 'directors' – it is their responsibility to engage in and add to the strategic decision-making process. Even one step removed from the Executive Board in large corporates, they will be expected to present their annual brand/business plan – which they are seen to 'own' – to the 'grown ups' at least once a year. Inevitably, they will have had help from other functions preparing this plan, but their ability to articulate and sell its commercial logic will be closely scrutinised – and its subsequent implementation even more so! For these reasons, outstanding ODs must do three things well under the aegis of this competency: provide *strategic clarity*, a *well-crafted purpose* and *aligned KPIs* that bring the strategy alive. These will be considered in turn.

## CLARIFIES DIRECTION

Outstanding ODs mark themselves out by setting out a viable 'joined-up' growth plan. This is a coherent strategic plan for their region/brand that tells people 'where' the region/brand wants to get to (vision), 'what' business it is in (mission), 'why' it exists for customers (purpose) – all backed up with a strategic route map which indicates 'how' it will achieve its objectives and KPIs over the long and short term.

> In small companies – especially – you have to elevate yourself from just the tactical day-to-day… you need to be able to see the wood from the trees; because whilst it's important to think about the 'present/here and now', you have to display 'holistic thinking' – focusing on shaping and delivering the organisation's long-term vision, mission and strategy because you spend more time with shareholders and investors.
>
> Gavin Smith, Managing Director, Pizza Pilgrims

It is a complex process – but the best OD strategies possess clarity and elegance, being:

- **Rooted in research** – they start with an in-depth appreciation of consumer behaviour and trends and a deep understanding of competitive forces
- **Collaboratively Formulated** – the strategic plan works best when it is worked up by and owned by the OD's team (most importantly the figures and budgets!)
- **Clearly Articulated** – successful strategies are clearly laid out, well-articulated and cascaded effectively throughout the brand/region (constantly being reinforced during face-to-face and digital communications)
- **Swiftly Implemented** – they are also acted upon and brought alive swiftly; quick wins are celebrated to maintain momentum
- **Always Adjustable** – as Mike Tyson said, 'every boxer has a plan until he's hit in the face'; strategies must adjust in 'mid-flight' to take account of new opportunities or seismic events (such as COVID).

Additionally, the most impactful strategies are built around difficult-to-replicate, 'inimitable characteristics', namely:

- **Distinctive Competencies** – the distinctive technical, behavioural and cognitive skills/talents already embedded in the region/brand. What are they? How can they be strengthened and exploited?
- **Strategic Assets** – the proprietorial physical, technical or portfolio-related resources, which have been built up over time, that are owned by the region/brand. How can these be more effectively leveraged?
- **Differentiated PODs** – the unique facets (or 'superpowers'!) of the region/brand's business model, offer and proposition which afford it competitive advantage; the ability to exploit a 'marketplace in a market space'! How can these be extended and protected?

*CASE STUDY 14 – STRATEGIZING FOR A 'BUSINESS WITHIN A BUSINESS'*

*Clive Chesser is the CEO of Punch Pubs & Co (1,300 leased pubs with a corporate headcount of 231, including an operational field structure of one MD, five ODs and 40 BDMs). Previously, Clive was OD and then MD of Greene King Pub Partners following spells at Enterprise Inns as an OD and Häagen-Dazs Cafes as International Franchise Director.*

Why is it important to set a long-term strategy as an OD, backed up with short-term goals? Because you have to create a *forward-looking culture* with a sense of uplifting purpose and vision for your field operators – both at an individual and the collective level. To that extent as an OD, what I tried to do was create a business within a business – without creating a divide. I would work with my team to set a vision backed up with milestones that were applicable to my region (within the framework, budget and aspirations of the company). This meant that what my people were doing – on a day-to-day basis – felt meaningful and relevant to their focus and endeavour. But how did I do it?

- *Team Contribution* – I have always had a strong sense of where I would like to lead my businesses; certainly, the commercial objectives coming from the centre are really clear. But to ensure we were the 'most professional, growth-focused region', I had to get the team involved in setting the *strategic priorities*, backed up with *tangible short-term goals*. Being inclusive (without submitting to excessive procrastination) only strengthens the will and resilience of the collective effort.

- *One Page!* – Having agreed the path, I have always done something that I regard as particularly important – setting it all down on one page! Operators are insanely busy people, with issues coming at them at a thousand miles an hour, day in, day out! In order to keep people's hearts and minds on the superordinate goals – preventing them from sinking under the minutiae – it's absolutely crucial that ODs have a strategic one pager (encompassing our regional vision, purpose, values, priorities and goals) that everyone can easily refer back to as their 'compass' on a daily basis. If what you are doing isn't on this page – don't do it; you are wasting time and money!

- *Stakeholder Buy-In* – In order to expedite the strategy, you have to co-opt resources and expertise from the centre. As an OD, you are often 'sharing resources' with other regions. Involving the central functions in the planning, communication and implementation phases of your strategy is key to its success. Why? *First*, you cannot execute your strategy without the input and help of key resource-holders. *Second*, by building up a great relationship with people at the centre you ensure that you always get the best service. In the past, I've had BDMs (some of whom were high performers that always hit the numbers) that have fostered combative and toxic relationships with the centre, but I will not tolerate this. We have to get stakeholders onside who share our will to win and actually want *us* to win.

- **Ownership** – In order to bring the Regional Strategy alive, I always – as an OD – expected my BDMs to present to me annually on their individual district strategies. This enabled me to check on their levels of alignment and their grasp of financials and commercial understanding. I have always viewed my BDMs as 'mini-MDs' of their own particular districts; they have to be able to articulate a vision and strategy as to how they will drive sustainable growth amongst their businesses – in keeping with the region's long-term and short-term aspirations.

What would I identify as bad and good OD practice in this area?

- **Bad Practice** – ODs that fall short in this area are habitually short-termist rather than long-termist in their behaviours. They are often obsessed with chasing bonuses or compromising long-term performance by winning holiday incentives. This is reflected in the way that they set up deals in short-sighted ways, with inappropriate people. They preside over 'boom and bust' agreements; this is expensive in an industry where the cost of business failure can amount to £20–40k per unit (depending on the size of the business). What they fail to understand is that leased and tenanted pubs are vital community retail and leisure hubs. Customers get annoyed when landlords revolve in and out of the doors of their local pub, resulting in a total destruction of local goodwill and huge micro-market share loss.

- **Good Practice** – ODs that do this well are able to reconcile both long-term aspirations with short-term priorities, without sacrificing either in their pursuit of business success. They gain a reputation as 'builders' rather than 'gorgers'. But in order to do so – as I have said at the top – they use all the talents of their team. I remember when I arrived at Enterprise from *Häagen*-Dazs; Northern Rock had just been rescued by the government and the world banking crisis was crippling businesses. I stood in front of my new team and said 'you are good at your jobs... you are the experts... I am looking for answers and solutions from you on how we are going to weather this crisis; and I will listen!' We ended up as the top-performing region that year, the only one to beat budget! A command-and-control approach (by someone who barely knew the pub industry) would not have worked in that particular situation – empowerment did!

So, to summarise, the best ODs are able to interpret what the needs of their organisation are and then synthesise and articulate a distinctive regional strategy and plan that is bought into and supported by all stakeholders. At a regional level, they involve their people in its formulation and then hold them to account for its execution. ODs that fake it or make it up as they go along – just aiming to hit next week's numbers – eventually come massively unstuck.

## *CRAFTS COMPELLING PURPOSE*

An important component of the strategic platform that the outstanding OD builds for their region/brand is the 'compelling purpose'. Why? If it is any good, it will be the one element of the strategy that their people remember and draw energy from on a day-to-day basis:

As a heritage business, largely dependent upon the success of our tenants (who we call 'business partners'), our purpose is to do everything we can to *'enable our business partners to flourish!'* It's quite simple – their success is our success. Everything we do must be geared to maximising their success. It's also something that motivates the team – because there is nothing more satisfying then seeing our business partners succeed – it gets people out of bed in the morning!

Stephen Gould, Managing Director, Everards

If ODs can't explain 'why' people should be there, they should forget it! Outstanding ODs will craft a compelling purpose with their team that possesses:

- **Easy Recall** – it is short, punchy and memorable (see the case study below)
- **Emotional Resonance** – it gives meaning to people, a feeling that they are engaged in a noble cause or worthwhile work that brings happiness and joy to customers; 'whomever you're trying to serve – make them feel it!'
- **Brand/Regional Ownership** – although it might imitate the corporate or organisational purpose, the most effective regional/ brand ones (although aligned) are customised and personal to the regional/brand tribe.

## CASE STUDY 15 – ENRICHING LIVES

*Karen Forrester was the CEO of TGI Fridays for twelve years, during which time she is widely acknowledged by industry experts as having orchestrated one of the great revivals within the history of UK hospitality (growing the estate from 40 to 86 stores, increasing EDBITDA from £4m to £30m). TGI Fridays was named at the top of the* Sunday Times *Best Companies to Work For list in 2015 and Karen was ranked in the top 50 of the* Caterer's *100 most powerful people in hospitality in 2018. Previously, Karen held senior field positions with other leading UK hospitality companies.*

Organisations need a purpose! Why? Because people need something to *emotionally connect* to – something with resonance and real meaning, that represents a *noble cause* or higher calling. In Fridays, our stated purpose was *'we enrich lives'* – for both our guests and team members. For guests, their lives were enriched by the *memorable experiences* we provided – the escape from humdrum everyday madness to a place where – for every minute they were with us – they were treated as *special*. For our team members, their lives were enriched by the *development, recognition and progression* opportunities we offered them, underpinned by a fun, progressive culture that made Fridays a great place to work.

But if I had to single out one thing that enriched lives above anything else at Fridays during my tenure, it was our *'earn your stripes'* ritual. When I took over in 2007, it had become apparent to me that this business had completely lost its sense of direction. For the first year or so, I knew I had to find one *totemic catalyst* to turn the ship around. The solution was presented to me by our teams, who kept asking me *'when are we going to get our stripes back?'* Both the US and UK had taken away their stores' 'stripes accreditation' (a process through which units 'earned their stripes' through intensive annual evaluations) because it was deemed too outdated. But I understood it wasn't about our people regaining their stripes per se, it was really a subliminal desire *'to get their pride back'*. The *symbolism* of stores being awarded stripes, due to achieving the highest quality standards, had been regarded as a *landmark event* by our GMs and teamers. But this opportunity had been taken away – morale had dipped, along with standards and attention to detail.

So a significant way in which we *'enriched our people's lives'* was by *'bringing back the stripes'* which – in turn – provided us with a real catalyst to turn around the *whole* business! And I can remember where it started: Newcastle. Having conducted refresher training with everyone and deep cleaned the site from top-to-bottom, we went in and tested everyone in order to *catch them doing it right* – and the store passed with flying colours and was awarded its stripes. We held a big graduation ceremony at St James's Park (photographing teamers being awarded certificates, pins, prizes, etc.) and from *that* moment on, sales in that store started to motor. And it happened everywhere else – a hockey stick rise in performance as *'united tribes'* in each store came together to raise their game to earn their stripes, followed by huge celebrations. Of course, we did other things such as returning the *Fridays DNA* to the food and drink offer (which had been diluted and dumbed down due to cost savings) and properly investing in amenity; but there is no doubt in my mind that the origins of rebooting this business lay in giving back our people their *identity, self-worth and personality* through reinstating their stripes.

How did my ODs over this period contribute to this? By being great advocates and cheerleaders for store stripes but *also* by adding further value:

- **100% 5\* *'Scores on the Doors'*** – levels of pride and commitment were enhanced further by one of my ODs who led the charge for Fridays to become the first restaurant chain in the UK to register 100% 5\* EHO ratings amongst its whole estate. He helped build the systems, processes and recognition mechanisms which galvanised the team to reach this highly stretching objective.

• **Sunday Times *Number One Best Place to Work For*** – another one of my ODs drove our aim to top the *Sunday Times* league table on the Best Place to Work For, by sorting out and *aligning* our communications and messaging. People were pulled together by *aligning our marketing calendar with our people calendar*; hence Mother's Day, family days, Valentine's Day, pets days etc. were also woven into employee recognition and communications mechanisms. In doing this, our people really began to understand (and could articulate) what our strategy, purpose and objectives were from the top to the bottom of the organisation.

So to my mind, both of my ODs drove important initiatives which validated and bolstered our *culture and purpose* at Fridays. And in this sense – both with the 100% 5* EHO and *Sunday Times* successes – both of these ODs were *trailblazers*. Too often in my career (especially before Fridays), I have seen ODs making 'zero sum contributions' by playing the corporate game; keeping it safe – controlling labour and just driving outputs. I want my ODs to think outside of the box – do something famous, leave a *legacy*! And at Fridays, I believe that's what they did.

## ALIGNS KPIS

In order to operationalise a clear strategy and compelling purpose, outstanding ODs will also (as stated above) give careful thought as to which tactical KPIs will – over the short term – keep them on course to hit their intended destination. This is often done badly by some ODs:

> Poor ODs just take the budget, carve it up, cascade it and then spend the year driving the outputs. They are obsessed with financial (output) KPIs, giving little regard to the input metrics that drive them (people, operations and customers). In my view, they blow up businesses – perhaps delivering short-term gains through cost cutting and crashing margins to drive sales. Outstanding ODs build balanced scorecards which tie all of

> the input and output interdependencies together and then (with corporate blessing) they incentivise their delivery. They accept the truism that what gets measured gets managed; but more than that, they understand that measuring and incentivising the *right* things leads to far more sustainable outcomes...
>
> James Pavey, National Operations Director, Tesco Cafés

Thus, in order to give their region/brand the best chance of short-term KPI delivery and budget achievement (paying out bonuses and incentives, lifting levels of morale and discretionary effort), outstanding ODs and their teams design and drive KPIs that are:

- **Balanced** – a mixture of both output (financial: sales, margin, cash-flow, labour and profit) and input (people engagement, operational excellence and customer satisfaction) interdependencies (see also 'Interprets Balanced Scorecard' in the 'Commercial Nous' competency below).

- **Aligned** – are congruent from the top to the bottom of the region/brand (i.e. at OD, AM, GM, DM, KM and Team Member level).

- **Achievable** – are stretching but eminently reachable; instilling confidence (particularly at the beginning of each KPI cycle) that people can 'blow the lights out'!

- **Timely** – have an element of monthly, quarterly, half-yearly and annual pay-outs to keep the 'pot on the boil' (without jeopardising the overall annual budgetary performance).

- **Targeted** – often ODs are masters at isolating and articulating the 'three things that really count' (i.e. NOMs/NODs at peak trading, shift/daily/weekly labour-to-sales ratios, staff productivity indices, customer satisfaction scores and/or employee engagement), ensuring that these are the measures that are articulated, incentivised and driven in the most important part of the business, namely: FOH/BOH team and shift level!

- **Appraised** – finally, the tracking and monitoring of KPI progress is subject to frequent appraisal and measurement so that remedial action (training, extra resources or correction) can be taken if people are falling short.

## CASE STUDY 16 – SETTING THE COMPASS FOR MY DIVISION

*Colin Hawkins has been a Divisional Operations Director for the Stonegate Pub Company for eight years, regularly winning regional and divisional performance of the year awards. Previously, he held regional, area and GM field positions with Mitchells and Butlers, Greene King and Sainsbury's. He graduated from the BCU Multi-Unit Leadership and Strategy Programme in 2012 with an MSc (with distinction).*

I believe that outstanding ODs understand and buy into the company's vision and strategy, *but* then work hard at articulating a distinctive Divisional identity and 'noble cause' which rallies their troops (whilst supporting the overarching organisational framework). For instance, I strongly believe that the success we have enjoyed over the past eight years within my Division (in its various guises) can be attributed to the way in which my team and I have set the compass; plotting a clear course which enables the wider area teams to really engage with the journey and focus their commercial energy. This is how I've gone about it:

- *Meaningful Vision* – when I started as a Divisional OD (with responsibility for over 200 units), I had a strong sense of where I wanted to take my team. I put a lot of myself into the Divisional vision. I didn't need anyone else to tell me to create it or that I needed it – it was to ensure my Division was to quickly become (and remain) *'the most admired management team within Stonegate'*. I believe it was aspirational and had a deep resonance. What I was doing was setting expectations for *my people* to be above the norm – imbued with a real visceral drive to outperform their peer group (both inside and outside the company).

- *Create a Narrative Brand* – what I wanted to do was create an elite team of hospitality professionals who took a real pride in worthwhile work. So what I created was a narrative brand within my Division, themed around the legend of the Spartans – the 300 elite soldiers (led by King Leonidas) who defeated the might of the all-conquering Persian army led by God King Xerxes in 480BC. The *symbolism* of this iconic victory – won against the odds by a small band of elite super soldiers – was then woven into all of my communications in the Division. We opened with a Spartan chant at our conferences, and at reward and recognition spots we put music on from the film *300* and crowned outstanding performers with Spartan helmets. We spontaneously recognised great performance at Unit level by issuing Spartan dollars that could be exchanged for cash, goods, holidays, etc. We have also held Spartan charity marches, runs and competitions. What it has done is create a strong collective identity, drawing on the clear virtues (honour, determination, pride, professionalism and mental toughness) displayed by historical legends over two millennia ago. It has bonded us as a team in our pursuit of the Divisional vision.

- *Clear Ways of Working* – at the same time as creating a strong sense of aspiration and identity, I needed to absolutely set my stall out in terms of conduct and standards. We created a Ways of Working document which required detailed signoffs at Unit level every six months. I spend an inordinate amount of time with new AMs, taking them though this document (which extends to detailing things such as email and voicemail etiquette) to ensure that they *do a proper job*. Why do I think this is essential? If you are slowed down by missteps on compliance, it paralyses creative energy and profit momentum. Getting it right first time gives you the time and space to really add value. In the words of Francis of Assisi, *start by doing what is necessary, then do what is possible, suddenly you are doing the impossible!* Or in other words: do the non-negotiables in the job, then hit the benchmark performance that is expected of your Area and/or Unit, and (suddenly) you have created a culture in which people have the mentality and opportunity to perpetually excel.

- *Define Strategic Focus & KPIs* – this is all backed up by a strategy to deliver what the company needs. I have always set four Divisional focus areas: three are 'continuous' (every year) sales, people and the company values; and one which is 'semi-flexible' – which (this year) was our customer service and engagement measure 'Great Serve' (GR8 Serve). All are linked back to the P&L and balanced scorecard but have distinctive Divisional angles and KPIs (i.e. sales – increasing post-8pm transactions) which are flexed on a yearly basis. Our focus areas are articulated through KPIs on noticeboards at Unit level and on the Divisional Facebook page, with Spartan dollar rewards being given out for things such as GR8 serve behaviours. But if I were to pick out the one KPI that really counts, it's quite simple: *like-for-like profit growth*. What I am aiming for here is not unsustainable gorging, slash and burn or 'skimming' behaviours. I want sound, sustainable, steady year-on-year growth based on 'good' rather than 'bad' profit. After all, anyone can buy customers (discounting) or cost-cut (savaging labour) and become a short-term hero!

In the end, my mantra is this: keep things simple! Create a strong, identifiable and aspirational culture which demands continuous commercial improvement. Accept the corporate profit challenge but find a way to imaginatively engage and inspire your people with things that mean something to them; inspiration that will turbocharge both required and discretionary commercial efforts. Hospitality is full of minimum-waged staff whom we ask a lot of, but I always say that it is the greatest example of a meritocracy – the rewards are there for the taking. If you want to work hard and get (as our CEO and Chairman have) from 'bar to boardroom', you can do it. But most importantly for our collective success, let's do a *'proper job'* and be *Elite Hospitality Professionals*. Let's be polished, professional and highly organised about how we go about our business at all times – and let's WIN!

# #5 COMMERCIAL NOUS

The next outstanding OD competency – ranked fifth by the twenty-seven senior interviewees – was Commercial Nous. This is the cognitive capacity to recognise, interpret and diagnose the key interdependencies between extensive quantitative/qualitative data sets. The personal qualities required for this include numerical reasoning, logical processing and higher-order critical thinking and evaluation.

At GM and AM level, commercial nous is required to understand the underlying financial dynamics of reasonably compact entities. At OD level, the complexity of understanding the commercial drivers of a far larger, varied portfolio with a vast P&L and a huge number of moving parts requires an exponential leap up in critical thinking and processing capability that some new appointees fail to develop.

> At district level you will have a bunch of units – in branded environments – that share fairly similar operational character-istics; albeit there will be a spread in performance. At regional/brand level you have a portfolio and P&L that will be anything from five to eight times as big. Often newly appointed ODs can get overwhelmed by the size of the task; confronted by reams and reams of information, they are unable to read the data and seize on the 'big rock' commercial insights that will help them to grow the business.
>
> Ric Fyfe, Operations Director, Gather and Gather

It is even more pronounced in multi-site unbranded managed formats and L&T environments – indeed, many of the senior L&T interviewees for this research exercise placed commercial nous in their top three outstanding OD competency requirements because:

> In L&T you need to be hugely commercially aware because you are dealing with a higher degree of ambiguity and complexity than in branded retail. Why? First, you don't have perfect information on the tenant's business – in spite of the fact that you might have sight of their books. Second, each business will be different – the balance of their P&L will differ according to scale, offer, market, demographics or capability. Third, you have to take large investment decisions to back tenants and projects that cover a multitude of propositions (from high-end premium to local community). Add into the mix that whilst – at BDM level – you had a pretty good feel for the sites, people and numbers, at OD level you are one step removed and you need to have developed a pretty sharp commercial radar to look at the data, reflect and make the right decisions!
>
> Mike O'Connor, Operations Director, Greene King Pub Partners

Clearly, being commercially savvy and *instilling a 'commercial culture'* in their regions/brands is a key OD skill, illuminated and highlighted by three specific practices identified by respondents, namely: *mastering the P&L, interpreting their balanced scorecard and 'reading' the region/brand's numbers.*

## *MASTERS THEIR P&L*

Outstanding ODs understand that – ultimately – they will be judged on their P&L performance, so their first port of call is to get on top of it and understand what it means.

> The first thing that an OD needs to do is understand the numbers! Why? Because that is the language of the Board and the grown-ups. That is the document they use to judge how your business is doing… so you better understand what each line is about. It sounds ridiculous but some AMs coming into the OD position have hidden their ignorance in this area; they have intuitively driven sales and converted profit – but they don't really understand concepts such as ratios, yields, margins, cashflow and depreciation, etc. And if you put a balance sheet in front of them, they wouldn't understand any of it.
>
> Elton Gray, Commercial and Operations Director, Creams Café

Their lack of understanding could be terminal. They will be embarrassed during brand/region profit reviews amongst senior people or get 'shafted' during budget cycles by unscrupulous bosses or finance managers! Outstanding ODs, on the other hand, get a grip on their P&L by mastering the:

- **P&L Lines** – they are conversant with every 'field' (both financial and ratio) on their P&L
- **P&L Calendar Year for the Region/Brand** – they have a complete understanding of the seasonal and calendar breakdown of their regional/brand P&L across the year (which gives them some sense of *'slack'* periods which they can attack)
- **P&L Break-Downs of Districts/Units** – they have drilled down to district and unit level to understand where the *'sleeve'* (or 'budgetary underloads') lie on their region/brand which they can sweat to compensate for the 'budgetary overloads' elsewhere.

*CASE STUDY 17 – THE IMPORTANCE OF MASTERING THE NUMBERS*

*Simon Longbottom has been the CEO of the Stonegate Group since 2014, building it up to become the largest pub company in the UK by 2020. Previously the MD of Gala and Greene King, he was elected to the Maserati 100 list of the UK's top entrepreneurs and crowned Leader of the Year at the Publican Awards in 2019.*

In the end, outstanding Operations Directors are judged by pounds, shillings and pence! Yes, they need to drive the inputs (people, standards, etc.) to get there but the bottom line is that they have to perform. If they want to reach 'Hero Operations Director' status, they have got to be seen by their peers and followers as performing year in, year out. Their start point? Really getting under the skin of their numbers and data.

Having run a number of big businesses and watched how some of my great ODs have mastered their numbers, I would offer two key observations as to how they do it. Firstly, they *stop and think*. They start with a *detailed analysis* of all their numbers (P&L, Budget, Investments, Balanced Scorecard, Key Exception Reports on Compliance, Customers and People). This is their start point; it precedes addressing the proposition and assessment of demand, competitive forces and the resources required to grow their business. But it ultimately informs all their actions in these areas, which is *now* based on sound analytics and diagnostics rather than guessology. These guys really get under the skin, understanding their ratios, gearing, margins, trends and areas of opportunity. But, secondly – and this is the most important factor – they are able to see the *wood from the trees*. ODs are faced with operational meteors 24/7; they've got to know what to catch and what to drop. It is this evaluation of their key priorities that requires a high level of deciphering skills. They've got to figure out from an extraordinary amount of data what the *key metrics and levers* are for their region/brand and then pull them aggressively to grow their businesses!

Not all ODs do this. Average ones can be one dimensional and over-index on areas of comfort. I've seen some ODs that keep gravitating back to a charismatic, inspirational leadership style and – in fairness – their team-engagement scores have been fantastic. But commercially they have been a disaster. Pursuing engagement at all costs and courting popularity by making bad commercial decisions – ultimately – drives their business down the pan. Other ODs that don't cut it on the numbers have probably been appointed through the ranks by displaying sheer graft and great hospitality skills, without metrics being part of their tapestry. This is fine on a small unit or area scale, but on a larger regional/brand canvas they get caught out. Often, I find that ODs who are frightened of the numbers need a commercial accountant at their side all the time (on visits and at meetings with me) to use as a 'prop' to answer my questions! The reality is that – whatever their personal qualities and drive – this fatal flaw will either be their undoing or will certainly prevent them eventually getting to MD level.

How do ODs develop the skill of mastering the numbers? To a certain extent, this is a *thinking skill* that can be learned; ODs who are willing to learn, working alongside outstanding ones, can pick up which reports and metrics count; what good looks like. Also, their MDs have a big role to play, coaching and developing them in this area. But the reality is this. The volume and pace of data generation in organisations is such that – going forward – there is going to be a far higher need for advanced cognitive thinking skills in this area. Sophisticated data-analysis skills will be an essential part of the OD of the future's armoury. A new dynamic breed of ODs (that I already see coming through) need to have the intellectual capacity to deal with the increasing size and complexity of their in-tray within hospitality. Take Leased and Tenanted, for example! Back in the day, pubs were let to tenants and ODs/BDMs made courtesy calls just to preserve the relationship. Now this sector of the industry is far more regulated and ODs need a greater commercial understanding of cashflow fore-casting and micro-market investment returns. This requires a deep financial analysis of lessee finances, increasing the complexity and commerciality of the role. Force of personality is not enough to run and optimise these businesses anymore!

So, mastering the P&L and the numbers is an absolutely essential starting point for outstanding ODs – particularly during this digital information revolution. When this is combined with great leadership skills, customer focus and a passion to win, it becomes a fearsome combination that – almost always, in my view – leads to commercial success!

## *INTERPRETS THEIR BALANCED SCORECARD*

In the competency ranked fourth above (Strategic Thinking), the respondents outlined how important it was to ensure key KPI inputs/outputs were aligned and articulated to drive congruent behaviours throughout the region/brand. In their pursuance, outstanding Operations Directors either worked off, or constructed their own, balanced scorecards:

> My balanced scorecard is really my key dashboard. What I am trying to do is ensure that – across my operations – I am achieving green (or at least amber) traffic lights on the key input/output metrics. But often it throws up a number of conundrums and paradoxes when you drill below the surface. Sometimes we can be smashing sales and have amber or red customer-satisfaction lights. This is what I call a 'lead' indicator. It leads me to ask: are we gorging on sales to the detriment of customer delight? Is it an early warning signal that customers will 'down tools' and go elsewhere unless we fix quality, speed, atmosphere, etc.?
>
> Alex Ford, Managing Director, Oakman Inns

Thus, outstanding Operations/Managing Directors like Alex Ford don't just take what their balanced scorecards say at face value; they scrutinise and interpret them, looking for any signs of:

- **Lead Indicators** – early warning signals on some parts of the scorecard that might impact other metrics in due course (e.g. poor employee engagement *now* will trickle through into poorer sales performance *later*).
- **Deadly Combinations** – in certain segments of the market, outstanding operators will be on the lookout for deadly combinations of metrics that spell massive trouble for their brands/regions (e.g. in 'value food', poor like-for-like sales scores combined with low customer satisfaction on 'price'; and in 'premium food', excessive drinks sales/declining food sales combined with poor customer satisfaction relating to 'quality, atmosphere and environment').
- **Conundrums** – sometimes there will be paradoxes, defying the laws of the Service Profit Chain, that will require deep-dive analysis, namely: high customer and employee engagement coupled with

declining sales. This is sometimes seen in brands with a loyal, die-hard cohort of customer 'zealots' who are 'holding out' in a brand veering off trend. An analysis of non-users, switchers or lapsed user opinion/behaviour would shed more light on this conundrum.

## CASE STUDY 18 – DRIVING THE RIGHT METRICS ON THE BALANCED SCORECARD

*James Pavey has been the National Operations Director for Tesco Cafés (315 units, 3,000 staff, two Operations Directors and 18 Area Mangers) since 2014. A veteran of the retail and hospitality industries, he graduated from the BCU's MSc in Multi-Unit Leadership and Strategy Programme in 2012 (with distinction).*

When I came to Tesco in 2014, many Tesco cafés were subcontracted out to Compass and Elior. Taking them back in-house, TUPE'ing staff over, we had a major job on our hands. This business was losing over £10m per annum and it was perceived as a major detractor within the wider Tesco family (our NPS stood at a measly 35%, at the time – way off Tesco Retail scores). Our new CEO (Dave Lewis, appointed in September 2014) made it quite clear from the off – publicly – that any part of the business that didn't generate a clean profit would be disposed of in his turnaround plans. By 2019, we had driven profit up to £20m. Putting in place a balanced scorecard that would drive the right behaviours was a key part of this success. How did we do it?

- **Define the Input/Output Metrics** – as part of the Tesco family, we followed the retail brand's priorities very closely:

  - *Safety (Operational Input) – a key metric on the Tesco Scorecard is customer safety; hence we set our EHO 'scores on the doors' aspiration at 5\* for all cafés.*

  - *Employee Engagement (People Input) – we set ambitious engagement scores so that we could transform the motivation of staff who had hitherto worked for third-party contractors.*

  - *Customer Satisfaction (Customer Output) – our aspiration here was to at least reach store retail levels of NPS.*

  - *Profit (Financial Output) – profit was the overriding mantra of the new regime so we set stretching targets which would ensure (first) survival, (second) sustainability and (third) expansion.*

- **Driving the Key Metrics** – next we drove the metrics on the scorecard, but paradoxically, not in the way that most businesses claim to do it! The two 'linked' metrics we hit hard were engagement (input) and profit (output). Why? Without engagement we weren't going anywhere. Without profit we would be disposed of. *Engagement* activities at the time consisted of:

  - *Regular communications Roadshows*

  - *Impactful and meaningful learning and development*

  - *Monthly communications cascades and webinars hosted by our MD*

  - *Team 5 (five-minute huddle) briefing packs and monthly notice-board poster*

  - *Annual Company Conference*

  - *Regular bi-annual manager–subordinate 'job chats' and 'check ins'*

  - *An aspiration to win the Retail Award's 'Café of the Year', which had been won nine years on the trot by Morrisons (and which we eventually achieved!).*

At the same time, we concentrated on creating a more *commercial, profit-focused culture* by restructuring reward packages for Team Leaders, Café Managers and Area Managers. Our new MD, Adam Martin – a highly respected hospitality marketing expert – drove the repositioning of our marketing mix (our proposition, product quality, pricing, place, etc.). The net result of concentrating on engagement and profit is that – paradoxically – they helped fixed the other two metrics on our scorecard! Safety metrics (EHO scores on the doors) rose from 3.1* to 4.97* in 2019. Customer metrics (NPS scores) rose from 35% to 71% across our businesses.

- **Impact** – the net effect of this is that, rather than being seen as an encumbrance for Tesco, we are now perceived as an important part of the wider business. We are also perceived as providing an extra point of service difference compared to the discount retailers (i.e. Aldi and Lidl). Future plans will probably involve expanding rather than culling our number of café units!

When I look back on my journey as an OD, I am glad that I had strategic experience of the role coming into the position. I had already made my missteps at this level elsewhere! Previously, I would have driven compliance balanced scorecard metrics and focused my attentions almost exclusively on the outputs (profit and customer satisfaction). But the key *dependency* on this scorecard – and I recognised it right from the get go – was to engage our staff and get some profit momentum! In turn, this would *increase pride* and move the compliance and customer metrics in the right direction. It would take longer, but I had the professional confidence to know the results would be more sustainable.

## DELVES DEEPER INTO THE NUMBERS

In addition to mastering the P&L and interpreting the Balanced Scorecard, outstanding ODs also display commercial nous by conducting their own independent deep number dives. That is to say, beyond the standard reportage they receive, they hunt for more internal data to understand what is really going on in their region/brand.

The standard reports you get as an OD can be quite top-line and superficial. What you need to do is dig deeper. What you go looking for is obviously influenced by the headline trends and signs you pick up from the P&L and balanced scorecards. But organisations with multiple functions generate a huge volume of data and you can also make your own customised requests. The best ODs don't just take a surface view; they are interested in delving into the *analytics* and getting in deep – surprising their bosses, peers and subordinates with their utter command of the minutiae and the important nuggets and insights they unearth that can really drive the business forwards…

Elaine Kennedy, Operations Director, Hawthorn
(The Community Pub Company)

So, what sort of deep-dive data do they go mining for to increase their analytical insight?

- **Historical Data** – many outstanding ODs won't just look at year-on-year data; they'll request reports that give them a real understanding of historical run rates (on sales, margins, SKUs, labour ratios, etc.) that will really give them a sound insight into trends and commercial/consumer behaviours. What happened in the business in the past – how does this inform us as to where it is today?

- **Exception Reports** – they will also delve into exception reports generated by Finance and the functions that might not be included as part of the management 'finance deck'. Exception reports such as pest-control visits, cellar and kitchen maintenance visits, and exit interviews will all tell their own story.

- **Bespoke Analytics** – also, as Elaine Kennedy highlighted above, really smart ODs will locate individuals around the organisation that can provide them with customised analytics on key issues they've spotted, but for which very little background data exists. This data will sometimes confound received orthodoxy on an issue, shining a light on the real causes rather than symptoms of a problem.

## CASE STUDY 19 – READING BEHIND THE NUMBERS

*Adrian Frid is the Operations Director for Caffè Nero UK (550 cafes, seven Regional Directors, 50 Area Managers and 2,500 staff). A veteran of the hospitality business – having started his career at unit level – Adrian was previously Operations Director of Miller and Carter.*

Clearly, having the ability to read the numbers is important. Reading *behind* the numbers is more important! Why? Regardless of whatever else you do, Operations Directors must be able to make commercial sense of how their businesses are trending. Taking a one-month snapshot is no good! Having done the role for over a decade now, Operations Directors must be able to diagnose what is going on quickly, in order to take rapid commercial decisions. How? These are the main 'watch outs' when I get in behind the numbers:

- **Abnormal Like-for-Likes** – the first thing I look for when reading the numbers is unusual like-for-like (l-f-l) patterns. If a store has a track record of consistent l-f-l growth over a number of years and then experiences abnormal decline, I like to look at a whole host of contingent factors that might assist my diagnosis. If *nothing has changed* in the store: has there been some economic shock in its local area? Has a competitor opened nearby? What should our response be? Quickly!

- **Unrepresentative Percentages** – I also don't get carried away by small stores that post improbably large l-f-l percentage growth. What's better: a small store that posts a 10% increase on 5k per week sales or a large one that posts a 3% increase on £20k per week sales (that washes through right to the bottom line!)? The latter is harder to do than the former. And certainly, the EBITDA contribution of the larger store dwarfs that of the smaller one. If I *get all my battleship-sized stores to trend at 3–5% l-f-l growth*, the business will take care of itself! Protecting these 'profit islands' is essential to the long-term health of the organisation.

- **Strategic Misalignment?** – I also bear in mind – when I digest all the figures – that we need to be aligned to company strategy. L-f-l sales growth might be great. But 'sales are vanity, profit is sanity!' What are the company's annual EBITDA growth requirements? What is the optimal cost structure of our business? Is what we are doing in line with Nero's three-to-five-year plan requirements?

- **'Serial Killer' Numbers** – I personally don't take any stellar growth in regional, district or individual stores at face value. I tend to look at all the metrics behind star sales/profit performers: their staff engagement (plus turnover and stability) and customer loyalty/satisfaction scores. Why? Because it is easy for field opera-tors to 'milk the business' (slashing variable costs) for short-term 'bonus gains' – *killing* the businesses they run before they move on. Therefore, I always scrutinise improbably good 'headline results' that are generated by 'serial killers', who can do untold damage to a business. But there will always be lead indicators and metrics which might help you stop their reigns of short-term gains before the damage gets too great.

- **'Force-Fed' Reports** – the other thing I do is sense check the numbers reports that are sent to me. For whom were they intended or designed? Are they of any benefit to me? If an exception report on marketing, supply chain, employees or property helps me to perform better – good – it'll rise up the ranking order with me. If not, I'll press the delete button. Sometimes I'll ask the providers of data and information to add extra lines in their reports that will add value to my understanding and commercial decision-making processes.

How do you develop the art and science of getting in behind the numbers? Speaking for myself, I didn't receive a university education in my youth (attending Harvard later on in my career) but I have always had the ability to find patterns and see pictures through the data. I can instinctively feel what is going on through the numbers and have developed the commercial nous to take quick actions based upon my interpretations. But don't get me wrong: the human dimension will always remain at the heart of everything I do and sits at the centre of Nero's culture. But in the end, if you can't read the numbers at this level, you (and eventually the business) are only going to go one way.

# #6 PROFIT IMPACT

The sixth rated outstanding OD competency – closely related to Commercial Nous (but more rooted in on-the-ground action rather than detached numerical analysis) – is Profit Impact. This is a laser-sharp approach to fixing underperforming parts of the portfolio (both at unit and district level) combined with a real talent for optimising asset investment. The qualities required for this competency are: courage, confidence, energy, proactivity and tacit operational knowledge.

Surprisingly, this competency and its associated qualities are not shared by all ODs:

As odd as it may seem, not all ODs have this visceral focus in confronting and resolving unit and district problems head on through direct action. Why? Some of them are too touchy feely – believing that cheerleading and greater engagement are solutions for everything. And – don't get me wrong – this transformational leadership certainly forms the bedrock of sustainable leadership. But there is a time and a place. Sometimes ODs have to roll their sleeves up and get stuck in to resolve the 'big bleeders' and faltering districts. Not resolving the issues by firing everyone but by really getting to the root causes on the ground. The best ones have a sixth sense for this kind of work and their value to organisations is vast. Moving assets and districts out of the bottom quartile of the Underperforming Assets Register (UPAR) is hugely beneficial to me and my top team...

Simon Longbottom, CEO, Stonegate Group

Clearly, as Simon Longbottom says, this competency is an essential part of the outstanding OD's armoury and something that they can build a formidable reputation for. In most organisations, 80% of senior operator time can be tied up in resolving problems in only 20% of the assets! ODs with this ability to speedily fix and find 'big bang' investment returns in their portfolio are a vital commodity in successful multi-site hospitality organisations – reducing their 'dragging tail' and 'sweating' their prime assets. How they do this in practice will now be considered in turn.

## *FIXES UNDERPERFORMING UNITS (UPUs)*

One of the common misconceptions of leadership is that great leaders shouldn't get too involved in the detail; they should build a talent pool around them and learn to delegate matters to relieve their burden. True to an extent; but outstanding ODs do not totally outsource the fixing of underperforming units (UPUs). Why? Because some of their largest battleships will constitute a disproportionate chunk of their budgets – several misfiring at the same time can have a calamitous effect on their capacity to hit their quarterly and annual profit numbers.

The reality is this. Prior to being an OD, I managed huge retail units for Sainsbury's and was an Area Manager – over a series of formats and concepts – for Greene King, Mitchells and Butlers, and Stonegate. Over the best part of three decades,

I have studied the art and science of optimising unit performance in any given situation. Going into units, I can usually feel within about half an hour what's misfiring by listening, looking and taking the temperature of the operation. Sure, I've looked at all the metrics beforehand – but nothing beats being on site, questioning people and 'feeling' the operation (its culture, atmosphere, standards, processes, offer quality, local positioning, etc.). Once I've established where the issues lie (product, proposition, people, place, processes, etc.?) I will establish an action plan with the AM and GM to turn it around in a tight timeframe with the appropriate resources and backing. I'll then reschedule a number of visits to check on progress. The one thing I always do is reserve judgement on whether the fault lies totally with senior site leadership. In my experience, too many operators in our industry reach for the gun too early. But few GMs *want* to fail. There is nothing better than to help someone who is experiencing hideous problems turn it around. It is often the making of them!

Colin Hawkins, Divisional Operations Director, Stonegate Group

Another reason why ODs get involved in underperforming 'big bleeders' is often – in spite of their best efforts – that the AM and their GM have been unable to track down the source issues because they are too close to the problem. Therefore, outstanding ODs are able to add value in this area by:

- **Seeing the Differences** – detached enough from the day-to-day operations, outstanding ODs are experts (as Colin Hawkins alludes to above) at seeing and feeling the differences. That is to say – with their tacit knowledge of unit excellence in most contexts – they can identify the gaps and opportunities which, if fixed, will result in better financial/cashflow performance.

- **Shaping the Remedial Plan** – but the best ODs also involve themselves in shaping the remedial plan. Why? Because they can often unlock valuable financial and human resources to accelerate the unit's turnaround (often by pulling down favours from Head Office).

- **Deploying the 'Turnaround Squad'** – in really extreme cases, the OD will have a go-to team on the region/brand who are their resident 'Turnaround Squad' that can be deployed to quickly fix things. Experts in various facets of the business (labour scheduling, food quality, marketing, pricing, etc.), they can lend quick assistance in whichever area of the business requires immediate attention.

## CASE STUDY 20 – TURNING AROUND UNITS

*Doug Wright DL, HonDoc, is the founder and CEO of Wright Restaurants T/A McDonald's Restaurants, currently operating twenty McDonald's franchised restaurants in the West Midlands (with a turnover of £80m, 2,245 staff, one Operations Director and four Area Directors). The Chairman of the Ronald McDonald House Charities in Birmingham, Doug was appointed a Deputy Lieutenant of the West Midlands and awarded an Honorary Doctorate by Birmingham City University in 2019.*

Outstanding Operations Directors have a high affinity for – and are *pivotal protectors* of – the brand. They are passionate 24/7 *ambassadors* for the business! Also, the best ones – alongside constantly spotting sales opportunities – create a *calm '360-degree ring'* around them that exudes an *aura*. The team believes in them and aspires to be like them – a *trusted* leadership role model who presides over a *winning, can-do culture*. Why is this so important in my business? Because effectively, my Operations Director is my MD. As I scout for opportunities to continually grow my business and ensure its long-term financial prosperity, my OD is my guiding operational light, driving the business forward on a day-to-day basis.

One critical role they have is maintaining the *optimal* performance of every one of our McDonald's units. Sometimes – in spite of our Area Directors' efforts (whom I regard as 'mini-MDs' in their own right) – individual unit performance can dip. How does my OD typically intervene and seek to minimise missteps?

- **Fix the Customer Journey** – taking a *customer-centric* approach, the first thing good ODs do is adopt a *'customer eye'*, closely scrutinising the FOH customer journey. Why? If sales are down and customer feedback is uncomplimentary, the first place to start is analysing problems through a customer optic. If the *customer experience* falls beneath expectations, they will then evaluate the most likely *'protagonists'*: people, product, process and place. And to fix the issues, they won't penny pinch; great ODs recognise that in order to turn things around they have to invest (in training, more staff, better amenity, fixing equipment, etc.). Because their sole aim is to transform poor experiences into excellent ones by restoring the intrinsic link between *happy staff and happy customers* – who are transformed from being 'non-believers' into raving advocates of the restaurant. The result: sales are driven back through the roof in the medium term!

- **Conduct the Orchestra** – in order to mitigate the chances of units misfiring, the OD has to ensure that all the parts *collaborate* with one another. To this end, they are a vital link between the functions at Head Office and the implementers on the ground. They can influence strategy, planning, organisation and resource allocation, having a profound effect on the short- and long-term performance of their units. In effect, ODs are a vital *check and balance* between the field and Head Office – *shaping* what gets fed down, whilst simultaneously *filtering* what is fed back up, to make the organisation more effective and successful.

I can remember one instance vividly when an OD of mine had a really important role turning around a unit. We had been given the opportunity to take over an underinvested franchise which, having bought it, we planned to refurbish after twelve months. We figured that although the décor was tired and the systems were outmoded, we could do enough to keep it ticking along until we invested after a year. But after a couple of days, my OD rang me and urgently requested a meeting. And I clearly remember him saying to me: *'Doug, we have to invest in this business now – we need to do something that demonstrates that we care for our new people and customers at this unit – we can't just plod along in this business!'* I thought about it and decided he was right. One month later, we closed and refurbished it and had two grand test re-opening's: one with our staff and their families, the other with local stakeholders and the community. And the response was amazing: *pride* returned to our people and the community became *energised and uplifted* by what we had done. I have always believed strongly that *community buy-in* and endorsement are vital for all of my businesses; if you want to be successful you have to make a difference in the community you operate in so that local people come to recognise the restaurant as *'my*

*McDonald's'*. Anyway – due to the drive and vision of my OD – this unit set off like a steam train; sales were transformed and it has since become a vital component of our portfolio.

So in summary, outstanding ODs can both jog and chew gum! They get the *bigger picture*, but they can also *roll their sleeves up* and resolve issues at the coalface. Poor ODs, in my view, just focus on the here and now, are reactive rather than proactive, don't empower their teams and always seem to *navigate around the root causes of problems* – until eventually the foundations fall in. Great ODs are the opposite: *inspirational leaders* that make decisions, trust their people and build *local* community-rooted businesses that will be sustainable over a three-to-five-year horizon.

## *RESOLVES UNDERPERFORMING AREAS (UPAs)*

A more challenging task for ODs is turning around underperforming areas. Why? ODs typically have (as the research for this book shows) anything up to eight AMs; if four of these are underperforming, they have a major issue on their hands. Turning around areas can be like turning around super tankers – the origins of their poor performance often being linked to:

> A losing mentality, *poor unit culture*, plummeting standards and lack of confidence in the AM who has totally lost the 'locker room'. Two key attributes that AMs need – in order to be successful – are credibility and dominance. With wide spans of control (typically up to 16 units in unbranded managed), there is plenty of opportunity for rogue GMs to undermine their authority and destroy their levels of influence. What does the OD do in this situation? Newbies to the position, who are struggling, can get there with some targeted OD mentoring and coaching – also with the OD pushing back against the AM detractors by showing his backing (in both word and deed). Remedial training and development can also help (using 360-degree feedback as the platform for addressing capability gaps). But often the OD doesn't have this time. Unless the underperforming AM takes a 'courage

pill' and has the tenacity to fight their way out, there is only one solution. Sometimes they are better off being moved to another area, where they can repair their reputation or take a move back down to GM. In some instances, they might take the advice that 'their talents might be better suited elsewhere in the industry'!

Elton Gray, Commercial and Operations Director, Creams Café

Demonstrably underperforming areas within the portfolio have other unintended consequences for the OD. They affect the reputation and morale of the wider regional/brand tribe – with questions being asked of the OD's mettle and capability. If regional/brand incentives are being diminished by a couple of serial underperformers, the malaise can spread! In reality – as Elton Gray outlines above – outstanding ODs can do three things to turn areas around (without doing the role themselves, acting like superannuated AMs!):

- **Coaching/Mentoring/Feedback** – having conducted a gap analysis of the area's performance, the OD gets the AM to take ownership for a detailed turnaround plan which they support through frequent, intensive one-to-one support.

- **Training/Development** – in order to plug particular capability gaps (established through rigorous analysis), the OD exposes the AM to immersive training and development interventions.

- **Sensitive Replacement** – but in the end – if things have got totally out of control – the best solution might be to grasp the nettle and move them on (either internally or externally). Finding an elegant internal solution is better, because few ODs want to gain a 'hire and fire' reputation amongst the wider AM population, with the job being as demanding as it is and a limited pool of multi-site management existing within the industry.

### CASE STUDY 21 – TURNING AROUND UNDERPERFORMING AREAS

*Susan Chappell is an Executive Director and Divisional MD of Mitchells and Butlers' City Division, which includes All Bar One, Browns Brasserie, Castle Pubs and Nicholson's. A thirty-plus-year veteran of the hospitality industry, Susan was previously OD for a number of brands, winning numerous internal company and external industry awards over the last fifteen years.*

As an OD, you cannot tolerate a severely underperforming area within your region/brand. Why? Firstly, it provides a massive drag on performance and causes a huge distraction for the whole team. It means that you can't really get beyond first base in order to get on with everything else you want to do: menu engineering, capital investments, sales and marketing initiatives, etc. In order to leverage the sexier things that will get you growth, you have to work off a solid platform – nobody wants to invest in a region or brand that doesn't have its house in order, so you have to take corrective action fast! Secondly, it has a negative effect on other areas within the region/brand – particularly if the OD is perceived to be ignoring or excusing this underperformance. Your other AMs and GMs aren't stupid; if they feel they are operating flat out and someone is holding back the performance, reputation and momentum of the region/brand, it saps their morale. 'Why isn't this being dealt with?' 'When is this going to be sorted out? Because it's embarrassing!'

In my experience, poor area performance always comes down to people. There will be excuses: 'new businesses have opened, stealing our customers', 'competitors are investing more in their offer and amenity' or 'a large turnover in GMs has destabilised sales and profit'. But when you dissect it, it's all about the calibre of leadership and capability on the area. It's not that they (the AM and key GMs) are necessarily bad people; it is the fact that they have let things get out of control – issues have piled up due to preventative or remedial action not being taken. The AM has appointed the wrong GMs with the wrong 'site fit' and stuck with appointments that just don't work, out of blind loyalty. Or, they haven't got the energy or courage to confront problems that are staring them in the face. As things spiral out of control on their area and the performance lag deepens, they start to panic or shut down.

How does the OD turn the situation around? (S)he has to make a full assessment of the situation, taking personal emotion out of their analysis. And in order to turn things around, the OD needs to display mental toughness, courage and compassion. It starts with tough, courageous conversations in order to get to the root causes.

Outstanding ODs – who are seen as credible, likable leaders – don't just fire people on impulse! They burnish their leadership credentials and create a loyal followership by being direct and honest with under-performers: setting out their expectations, contracting with them (with agreed goals and milestones) and providing intensive coaching as back-up to get AMs and their districts to where they want them to be. Obviously, different approaches might be needed for different situations. In some cases, AMs have been appointed from GM too early, so accelerated development might be needed. With 'lifer' AMs, who have been on a patch for too long (five years generally being the optimum amount of time), they might require a reboot by moving on to another district. For those AMs, however, who have failed to move with the times – constantly resisting change and rejecting the necessity to learn and take on more skills – more drastic action might be needed.

But what does good and bad OD practice look like in this area?

- *Dithering and Drifting* – there have been some instances when I have seen (generally new) ODs back underperforming AMs, because they have come in saying 'the slate is wiped clean and I want to give everyone a chance'. This is fine. But if they don't back this up with clear short-term goals and targets, they are instilling a false sense of security in some AMs that think they are doing an OK job (in spite of missing all their scorecard targets). If they haven't immediately contracted with the AMs and districts that need 'lifting' and had those courageous conversations with individuals (couched with offers of support), things will only continue to drift south – jeopardising the OD's position!

- *Talent Building* – often, a poor OD sticks with underperformers because they don't have sufficient talent lined up to strengthen their region/brand in key positions. Outstanding ODs are brilliant at attracting, developing and retaining talented people who they can shift around their region/brand to build traction and success. Because, ultimately, if poor district performance is down to people – and in my view, it is, 90% of the time – the solution lies in having highly motivated, capable and passionate people all over your region/brand to plug the gaps, rebuilding, rebooting and sustaining high performance in areas that might have previously acted as a massive drag on performance.

So in summary, it's all about people. The hospitality business is all about creating experiences and memories for our customers; you need fired-up teams and districts that provide this. Areas lacking leadership and a strong vision have to be turned around – quickly. But any changes have to be made both courageously *and* with compassion. I have often found that good people are possibly operating in the wrong space; a new lease of life in another unit or area with a better fit can really help people to turnaround their personal performance. But you have to have built sufficient bench strength up in your region/brand so that you can put all of the pieces of the jigsaw in the right place at the right time to create the right results!

## LANDS INVESTMENTS

Another important practice relating to the demonstration of this competency (Profit Impact) is landing investments. Multi-site hospitality requires the significant annual deployment of sunk capital to build, refresh and reposition amenities (in order to keep on market or satisfy new trends). Outstanding ODs are experts in optimising ROI returns for the investment monies they have either been allocated or tendered for in Portfolio Capital Meetings:

In my view – in L&T – this skill is absolutely essential. You will have a diverse portfolio of assets and a bunch of business owners who will all have great ideas on how they can improve their businesses through 'joint-capital' investment in their buildings and infrastructure. The difference between outstanding ODs and the rest is that they can discriminate between 'high-risk capital' and 'smart capital' that drives superlative growth. Their ability to evaluate what really drives growth – through capital investment – in any segment of the market (community, tavern, destination, etc.) is finely tuned and sophisticated. They don't just hose capital away for the sake of it.

Stephen Gould, Managing Director, Everards

In addition to having, as Stephen Gould says, 'finely tuned' sensitivities, outstanding ODs are effective at landing investments by:

- **Knowing their Portfolio Opportunities** – really understanding where 'hidden value' lies within their portfolio, through an in-depth understanding of their estate. Outstanding ODs in L&T with hundreds of units develop an encyclopaedic knowledge of their regional assets quickly. When proposals are put to them by BDMs, they will be able to visualise (based on their knowledge) whether or not they pass the initial 'smell test'. In addition – in large corporates – they are adept at 'transferring out' slack assets that can be exploited more effectively elsewhere in the wider corporate portfolio or making the case for underexploited assets to be 'transferred in' from elsewhere (say from L&T to Managed or vice-versa) by accurately sizing and delivering profit upside on a consistent basis!

- **Sizing the Right Capital Injections** – as stated, experienced ODs will also have a broad idea as to what any amount of capital, in any given site/format, will yield them in absolute terms. This is both an art and a science; but often in community assets, small FOH sparkles will throw off as much ROI as a bigger project with bolt-on 'hidden' BOH costs. In premium units, however, larger, bolder injections of capital might yield more effective results than just painting the windows and replacing the carpets.

- **Picking the Right Team** – the preference for most ODs would be to land investments during seasonal down-times or at the beginning of the financial year so that they optimise returns. In any event, all projects – once committed and started – need to be landed at speed: closed units cost money! For large capital projects (involving a significant repositioning of the unit), outstanding ODs will have deployed excellent pre-opening resources that assist the GM (with the right energy, experience and site 'fit') and his team to open successfully. The mark of a great investment being not its first month's trading, but its performance six-to-twelve months down the track! Additionally, it is important to state that outstanding ODs will *never* combine high-spend investments with external GM appointments. Both are high-risk actions – to do both at the same time is (as Simon Longbottom commented to me in his interview) a sure-fire way of buying a ticket to 'crazy land'.

## CASE STUDY 22 – OPTIMISING PORTFOLIO INVESTMENT

*Adam Fowle was Senior Non-Executive Director of the Ei Group (4,400 leased, tenanted and managed pubs) until its sale in February 2020. Previously, he was Chairman of Tesco Hospitality, Non-Executive Director Bistrot Pierre, CEO of Mitchells and Butlers, the Retail Director of Sainsbury's and Executive Director, Bass Leisure (where he founded Hollywood Bowl).*

Outstanding ODs really understand the importance of optimally investing in their portfolio's physical assets. Why? *First*, from an economic point of view, they get the fact that any cash that is given to them by the company (certainly for expansionary investment) has to exceed WACC (weighted average cost of capital available on the markets). Also, from a mathematical point of view, it has to produce a positive ROI (exceeding 20% in most companies) so that it pays back well within the standard investment cycle (usually seven years). If they do not have a mastery of the figures and their macro-effect upon the company's cashflow and growth aspirations, they shouldn't be doing the job! *Second*, from a customer perspective, hospitality is an extremely competitive market with low barriers to 'customer switching'. Assets are perpetually 'cash hungry' and, as one of my best ODs once said to me, 'I can't keep growing you like-for-like sales with like-for-like amenity decline!'

But how do the best ODs invest in their estates?

- **Understand Investment Goals** – great ODs understand the difference between *maintenance* and *expansionary* capital. Maintenance spends (such as 'sparkles') are designed to maintain and defend assets, being depreciated out of the asset over time. This should be used judiciously and carefully to provide the consumer with a consistently excellent 'physical experience'. Overspending in this area, when you will not necessarily grow the business (rather keep what you've got!) is an important factor to bear in mind here. On the other hand, expansionary capital – greater in size – needs to be researched, justified (usually to a Portfolio Allocation Committee) and then scientifically applied for optimal returns.

- **Understand Assets** – but in order to put the right amount of cash in the right formats, in the right assets, to generate the right returns, the OD really must know his/her portfolio and individual assets. When I visited prospective investment sites with the best ODs, they really understood the competitive and demographic dynamics of the sites' local micro-markets. They had used intelligence from multiple sources – their Area Manager, Property Portfolio Managers and Marketing – to build up a picture of what an optimal investment might cost and how a cast-iron payback was going to be derived.

- **Understand Operational Accountability** – in addition, when big investment projects kicked off, the best ODs had already moved in an operational team (AM, GM and 'house') that would run and be involved in the project from beginning to end. I've seen ODs move 'investment impact' AMs and GMs around to open projects and then pull them, handing over to newly appointed operators. This doesn't work. The most capable ODs understand that *accountability* from start to finish by those who will open the newly invested unit and 'own' the subsequent budget is the key to success. Sometimes, they will have to *sensitively* change the unit team, prior to the investment being committed (due to people–brand/format mismatches) – but this is sometimes a necessary move. The unit team must fit the proposition and customer demographic if it is to succeed.

- **Understand the Costs of Closure** – also, the best ODs really get the fact that time closed diminishes the rate of return in that calendar year. If the investment is done early in the year or during a slack month, the unit can gain momentum or avoid serious profit leakage. Good ODs optimise the benefits of closing and opening at the right times in a masterful fashion.

Where it all goes wrong is when ODs spend on vanity projects, aiming to be the OD with the biggest, smartest pubs. They don't understand the difference between investing for scale or investing for growth. Smart ODs avoid investing in big declining assets in the wrong places – rather, they deploy capital in assets that have obvious growth potential. Also, some poor ODs I have watched allocate capital to favourite AMs or units in areas that they have some (misguided) affection for. In addition, in some sites, some ODs are prone to 'overdoing it' – pissing away capital on 'additional works' that will yield no tangible return. They might also – in many cases – underestimate (or fail to factor in) contingencies such as expensive back-of-house costs. The best ODs don't do any of this. They've got all the bases covered and, generally, always outperform their peers on investment return metrics – year in, year out!

# #7 PLANNING AND ORGANISATION

The outstanding OD competency that ranked seventh was Planning and Organisation, which is the ability to schedule, prioritise, delegate, monitor and project manage. It is a critical skill in dispersed multi-site hospitalities organisations where it is impossible to evaluate site execution on a 24/7 basis. The skills and qualities required for this competency include structured thinking, time management, thoroughness, dominance and persistence[11].

Given the importance of multi-unit hospitality units operating in a safe, hygienic, standardised way – to a consistently high quality – why is this competency only ranked seventh? Possibly because it was taken as a given by the senior interview respondents for this book that most ODs have excellent planning and organisation capabilities, coming mostly as they do from managerial multi-site AM positions where they have already mastered this particular competency. In addition, they are greatly helped to cover off this competency requirement by other functions in the organisation such as Audit, Marketing and Operational Excellence.

But do all ODs really display either an affection or capability to plan and organise well? The reality is that a lot of ODs despise detail – they are far more interested in the sexier aspects of running their businesses. In truth, many ODs outsource much of their planning and organisation activities to Belbin 'planner-type' AMs on their team or co-opt the help from people at Head Office. A smart move? Not necessarily:

---

11  For wider reading on driving operational excellence, see 'Coaching Leaders to Grip Operations' in Edger, C., and Heffernan, N., *Advanced Leader Coaching – Accelerating Personal, Interpersonal and Business Growth* (Oxford: Libri, 2020), pp. 177–92.

> In tightly defined brands, I wouldn't expect our OD to be our smartest strategic thinker but I expect them to have the planning, organisation and executional capability of their region nailed on. I expect big calendar events that are 12–18 months out to be well thought through and resourced. Why? Because one small change on the menu – for instance – has huge ramifications... changes in recipes might have significant labour consequences. So I most certainly expect my ODs to become accountable and get into the detail.
>
> Karen Forrester, ex-CEO, TGI Fridays

So – clearly according to Karen Forrester – in distant, fragmented multi-site hospitality operations, accurate planning and *creating a culture of relentless execution* are the hallmark of outstanding OD practice in order to enforce standards and implement key initiatives flawlessly. These will now be considered in turn.

## ENFORCES STANDARDS

In the most important competency – Leading to Win – respondents highlighted how outstanding ODs communicated well and constantly 'modelled the values'. Effectively, they set the tone of the region/brand through their expectations for high standards – defining and driving a passion for an *operational excellence culture*. In fact, they regard it as a hygiene factor, a 'pay to play' element of their operations. Nobody gets off first base unless they consistently execute the brand/format blueprint day in, day out:

> The starting point is ODs want to go to sleep at night! Are their operations safe and secure for customers and staff? Are staff abiding by health and safety and licensed premise/ gambling regulations? Also are the units kept to a sufficiently high operational standard? Do their FOH and BOH operations conform to the organisational or regional/brand standard? Do their people actually care about the importance of consistently high execution? Outstanding ODs will have positive answers to these questions. Poor ones won't!
>
> John Dyson, National Operations Director, Mecca Bingo

In pursuance of achieving consistently high standards, hospitality organisations will generally have excellent induction, training and refresher programmes (delivered online and face to face) which will assist the OD's mission to achieve operational excellence across their region/brand. In addition, the best ODs will have earmarked exemplar 'Houses of Excellence' to showcase best practice and provide development to newbies and those requiring remedial training. But high levels of hospitality staff turnover, continual squeezes on labour deployment and poor on-site leadership, combined with the high intensity of some operations, are constant threats to operational execution. Clearly, their AMs will have a critical role in ameliorating such threats, but the outstanding OD will provide additional reinforcement through:

- **Defining the Blueprint** – having a hand in drafting and/or improving the operational standards blueprint so that they own it and signal its vital importance.
- **Setting Expectations** – setting high expectations for quality standards by *embedding them in the culture* of the region/brand, constantly communicating how important they are to them as a base 'hygiene factor' for performance.
- **Unannounced Visits** – making structured and unannounced visits so that they can keep people on their toes and 'catch people doing it right'!
- **Rewarding Excellence** – recognising and rewarding AMs and units that consistently post high OER (Operations Excellence Review) scores.

## CASE STUDY 23 – ENFORCING CONSISTENCY AND INTEGRITY

*Elton Gray is the Commercial and Operations Director of Creams Café, a national chain of dessert and gelato parlours (91 units – ten managed and 81 franchised – 68 franchisees, one Area Manager and four Franchise Support Managers). Previously, he held senior field positions with Strada and YO! Sushi after completing BCU's MSc in Multi-Unit Leadership and Strategy Programme in 2012 (with distinction).*

Enforcing the franchise blueprint is by far the biggest challenge for any franchisor. Some franchisees will always 'push the envelope', departing from the pre-specified brand standards to try and serve their own best interests – for instance, breaching terms by sourcing 'cheaper' but inferior ingredients elsewhere or buying less expensive machinery or technology that is manifestly unfit for purpose. As the Operations Director for a fast-growing brand, I cannot permit this to happen. Why? Consistency of our offer – throughout all our dessert parlours – is absolutely vital for our momentum and existence. A few rogue stores that 'freeride' the brand's reputation or 'skim' the terms of the franchise agreement can do untold damage to your brand. Their maverick behaviour undermines the 'system scale benefits' we offer to franchisees (product from our Dagenham production, sales and marketing support, preferred equipment supply agreements, etc.) and destroys the credibility of the franchise fee. Potential franchisees researching our brand (online and on the ground) will spot the cowboy operators within the system, questioning the integrity of the brand and what it purports to offer.

How do I ensure that standards are upheld and our franchisees religiously stick to our brand blueprint? *First*, all franchisees sign an extensive *franchise agreement* and can be held to account if they depart from the agreed terms. In some instances, we can 'breach' people out for non-conformance – and we do, albeit with a conscience (diplomatically and sensitively). *Second*, we now only *recruit* franchisees that fit our brand profile, whom we adjudge sufficiently attuned to our *culture and procedures*. *Third*, our *induction* processes now involve extensive blueprint training where prospective and new franchisees are totally immersed in our rules, procedures, systems and ways of working. *Fourth*, we have devised an extensive suite of *training packages* that franchisees can take to refresh their skills and knowledge in areas that might be lacking. *Last*, I have changed our *'functional' monthly brand audit* procedures – where we 'policed' the parlours! – into more *'customised' operational excellence checks*, where our Franchise Support Managers monitor and coach according to differing levels of capability. Some of our franchisees have other franchises with other companies and might have their own support infrastructure (Area Managers, Auditors, etc.). They need less support than a single franchisee that has come to us with minimal experience of running a hospitality franchise.

I can think of two examples where we have had to 'bring people back to centre' on brand standards and procedures with some success:

- **Luton Turnaround** – this parlour has recently been sold on by the franchisee (generating a healthy profit!) but was in a pretty ropey state when I got involved a while back. This was one of our original concept units and things had fallen into a state of disrepair. Kit wasn't being fixed (the waffle machine had packed up) and the unit was running a pared-back menu. *I visited the unit with a purpose*, explaining the standards required and what a 'return to quality' would reap in terms of return. As we have ten company units, I can showcase to franchisees the benefits that running parlours to specification can bring! Two weeks later, I returned and the franchisee – having implemented some of my suggestions and requirements – was starting to see the benefits. People were coming back into the store and delivery sales were up.

- **Leamington Expansion** – this parlour is run by an exceptionally talented businessman who – before I joined the brand – felt that unnecessary changes were being made to the brand, compromising his sales. *Trust* had evaporated and this franchisee wanted to exit the system. But having sat down with him and listened, also explaining why some of the changes were required and giving him assurances that his input would be sought in future changes, I started to rebuild our *relationship* with him. He is now totally onboard with the brand, with aspirations to expand by opening two or three parlours in other adjacent territories.

In the end, you do have to strike the balance. In order to counter franchisee perceptions that you're profiting solely from their 'sweat equity', you have to demonstrate real added value to the business relationship. It has got to be *win–win*: with the *franchisor* proving – day in, day out – that the franchise and royalty fees being paid by the franchisee are justified through the provision of best-in-class support and services; and the *franchisee* fulfilling their side of the bargain by adhering to the *brand standards and culture* for the benefit of the whole system. Our aims are mutual: if we both keep to our sides of the bargain, we keep growing *and* you will grow with us!

## *IMPLEMENTS PLANS*

In addition to reinforcing standards as a fundamental foundation of the region/brand's operational capacity, outstanding ODs also demonstrate foresight and forensic preparation for key calendar initiatives and events. Whether these initiatives originate centrally or locally, outstanding ODs carefully schedule, prioritise and resource their planning and execution:

> The careful planning of seasonal 'big days', sporting events, promotions, price changes, drinks offer or menu changes, etc. cannot be underestimated by ODs. Planning and organisation sit at the heart of all successful operations in multi-site companies for synchronous impact. That is why I say that great ODs are fantastic at 'managing the chaos' – creating structure and focus in highly volatile circumstances. But if you can create some semblance of orderly planning and control, it gives you space to do other things, such as experimentation and evolution of the offer…
>
> Helen Charlesworth, Executive Managing Director,
> Stonegate Group

As ODs grow into the role and transition through a few annual cycles, they become better at anticipating and correcting any school-boy errors that usually arise from poorly planned central/local sales drives or cost-saving initiatives. But in general, the best ODs are effective in this area because they:

- **Prioritise Big Rocks** – outstanding ODs are fantastic at prioritising and landing initiatives that will really benefit the P&L. They recognise that (in spite of Head Office's naïve expectations) the 'bandwidth' in their region/brand is limited and the operational line's preference is growing sales. It is better to concentrate on landing the big sales initiatives impactfully, rather than beating everyone up to do everything on the calendar perfectly.

- **Strategically Delegate** – in addition, outstanding ODs will have strategically delegated key processes and activities out to AM 'leads' and 'champions' who have demonstrated expertise in a respective discipline. They will devote the time and attention to ensure that certain initiatives are launched across the region/brand on-time and to specification.

- **Locally Customise** – also, great ODs won't accept central plans at face value: they will insist on a degree of local customisation (early on in the planning process) that will increase their chances of success.

## CASE STUDY 24 – TRANSLATING GOALS AND STRATEGICALLY DELEGATING PLANS

*John Dyson is the National Operations Director for Mecca Bingo (77 Clubs, 2,500 employees, six Area Managers) owned by Rank Plc, also the owner of Grosvenor Casinos and significant online gaming businesses. He is a 2013 graduate of BCU's MSc Leisure Leadership and Strategy Programme (with distinction).*

I see one of my primary roles as *articulating and translating* company goals into Mecca brand plans, then prioritising actions, forming plans and delegating them out amongst my wider team. To that end, my objective is to provide *direction* and *clarity*, energising and coaching a team of high capability and resilience to execute plans that provide real *traction* for the brand. Our overarching corporate goal? Mecca is fighting its corner in a particularly challenging space in the leisure market; providing safe, thrilling, memorable experiences for customers, which *grows footfall* in local micro-markets (because clubs are viewed as local amenities, rather than being viewed as part of a national entity), is absolutely critical. All our plans and efforts must be directed to that superordinate goal. It is my job to ensure total focus and precise effort around any plans designed to achieve it.

How do I turn our corporate objectives into reality? First, I am close to central decision-making processes, sitting on the Operations Executive for the company. Second, I have a daily call with my team at 11.30 a.m. where we discuss and monitor progress on various plans and initiatives, also considering any new priorities. These plans and priorities are generally delegated out to my direct reports who will lead or be involved in multi-functional workgroups (with marketing, slots, HR, legal, property, etc.) to land value-added initiatives that will either keep our clubs safer or grow our revenue streams. But we cannot do everything! My job is to ensure that people do not suffer from overload. I have to make sure that, when I delegate tasks out, my team has the bandwidth to cope. What do I mean by this? That they have both the time and skillset to cope with what they are being asked to deliver. To that end, I try to *strategically delegate* the right tasks to the right people (in both the AM and GM population) rather than just shovelling extra work onto people who can't cope. A couple of recent examples that demonstrate this spring to mind:

- ***Growing Events and Entertainment (E&E)*** – one of the great advantages we have in Mecca is space. The greatest challenge we have is sweating this space outside of core bingo trading sessions. What I did here was delegate an E&E workstream to one of my AMs who is particularly energetic, creative and charismatic. At first, he tried to do it all on his own, but – over time – with coaching and mentoring, he has taken a more collaborative approach, drawing on resources from marketing etc. He has also had to think more strategically than tactically. Will this concept work nationally rather than in just six clubs? Or can things be rolled out nationally, with the ability to customise products on a local basis? I don't want loads of local 'one offs' that disproportionately draw down resources and energy! And he has been successful, launching products such as 'bonkers bingo' and 'rewind festivals'. Right person, right attitude, right task, right approach (with some coaching!).

- ***Safer Gambling Compliance (SGC)*** – to a certain extent, bingo is further off the radar than other gaming activities. It is a supervised, low-stake wagering activity where we can monitor and track unhealthy addictive behaviour. However, I am determined that we cover any danger spots here: we have to ensure that all of our customers are gaming responsibly, without endangering their mental health or putting their financial security at unwarranted risk. So, I delegated the SGC workstream to another AM, a calm, methodical, diplomat who had great links with the compliance team at Rank. What I tasked him to do was translate the 'legalise' of our RGC responsibilities into plain, day-to-day operational language. And he has been successful. In the past, if you asked a Team Member what they did, they would have said 'I work in F&B' or 'I work on the books', etc. Through the simple training programmes and messages this AM has devised with HR, our Team Members now say 'I *look after customers* by doing the following...'. They now state a *duty of care* for customers as being their primary objective, rather than just their job role!

So translating company goals and aspirations into tangible value-added plans is one of my main roles to ensure clarity, alignment and impact. But I learnt early on in this job that I can't do everything on my own; and if truth be told, planning and organising aren't my greatest strengths! But I have learnt that crafting plans, strategically delegating them out and then monitoring progress through a regular communication process really does work. The key point being that I focus efforts upon shifting 'big rocks' rather than throwing 'small pebbles'!

## FACILITATES CHANGE

There are generally two types of change within organisations: transformational and incremental[12]. The former usually has deep structural and cultural ramifications – initiated as a reaction to external events that threaten the business model and/or a change in senior leadership. The latter – incremental change – results from an organisation's need to keep on-trend by evolving its offer, technologies, systems, processes and procedures. Inevitably, transformational change is harder to inaugurate than incremental change, because of the threat it poses to entrenched vested interests within the organisation. In fact, humans are naturally predisposed to baulk at any change, which means:

> ODs have a massive challenge on their hands getting the line to change the way it does things! Why? People have taken a long time getting used to a new rostering or service delivery system – for instance – that they were told was the bee's knees; and then they might be told that it's not quite right and everything needs to be changed again! Often the changes have been imposed centrally with little consultation with the OD and their team. So what does the OD do? Bad ones just passively do nothing or actively try to blow things up. Good ones have the guile to slightly adapt things and – ultimately – make it work for their team and region…
>
> Ric Fyfe, Operations Director, Gather & Gather

12  For wider reading on leadership and change, see 'Coaching Leaders to Spark a Change Culture' in Edger, C., and Heffernan, N., *Advanced Leader Coaching – Accelerating Personal, Interpersonal and Business Growth* (Oxford: Libri, 2020), pp. 192–209.

Outstanding ODs accept that change will be a constant factor during their tenure of operational leadership! The best ones:

- **Apply Patch Ups/Workarounds** – outstanding ODs either get in early and meld changes to the needs of their brand/region or – if they've been totally ignored – apply subtle patch ups and worka-rounds to what they've been given to satisfy 'the spirit if not the law' of the changes.

- **Upsell Benefits/Create Buy-In** – having put their own individual stamp on the change, they then go about upselling its benefits in terms of increased sales/productivity or decreased costs, being constantly mindful of avoiding the accusation that they are merely polishing a turd.

- **Generate Quick Wins** – most importantly, they demonstrate the efficacy of the changes by communicating quick wins that have either generated more sales or saved time, money and effort.

- **Don't Let Up!** – finally, with so many change initiatives withering on the vine in organisations through fatigue and overload, they sustain the momentum on value-added change initiatives by frequently rewarding and recognising their successful execution.

## CASE STUDY 25 – URGENTLY DRIVING CORPORATE CHANGE

*Jon Walters is the Operations Director for Qbic Hotels, a start-up 'hipster' premium boutique hotel chain backed by Cerebus. Previously, Jon held senior field operations roles with Premier Inn and is a 2017 graduate of BCU's MSc in Multi-Unit Leadership and Strategy (with distinction).*

When I was at Premier Inn, all corporate change – requiring imple-mentation through Operations – was seamlessly designed and project managed by the centre. Here at Qbic – a relatively new start-up attempting to exploit the 'hipster' niche of the hotels market – I am the corporate change centre! I have been brought in at a fairly early stage of development (we have three hotels – with a pipeline of eight more pending) to systematise operations but without a great deal of central support. Why is constant change and refreshment needed in this early part of its roll-out? Because even in the initial stages, if you don't learn and evolve as you grow, you will die!

In order to keep competitive, we have to do three things: ensure our *safety and standards* are best in class, our *employees* are highly engaged and our *customers* love our urban lifestyle hotels! When I arrived, we were doing some things well in these areas, but many things have required urgent attention. To that end, I have had to identify what we need to change and then design it – mapping it end-to-end. Then I have had to identify who in the organisation might have the 'developable' skills and competencies to land the change, and the willingness/readiness to do it. Following this, I have had to communicate out the change initiatives to get as much buy-in across the company as possible (by inspiring people and creating early adopters) – then drive the assigned individuals and small teams (through lots of little meetings) to land and implement key initiatives. I'm afraid that until you build a wider bench strength of capability, this level of micro-management is always necessary in start-ups, until people have grown enough to do it with less supervision.

Two change initiatives were driven by me early doors as a matter of both urgency and necessity:

- ***Operating More Safely*** – when I arrived, I realised pretty quickly that I needed to overhaul the hotels' safety and security proce- dures (so that I could sleep at night!). I put a paper to the CEO which was approved, engaged a health and safety company I had used at Premier Inn, agreed a brief and then got one of my senior managers to take it over as a project. Our aim? To ensure we were absolutely watertight on every aspect of health and safety proce- dure in relation to the operations of our hotels. I worked closely with this manager, communicating and implementing the plans and procedures designed by our health and safety consultant. But at times, things kept falling over. We kept working on a circle of continuous improvement until we got it right. To a large extent, it was not just about procedures but also about *changing the culture*. And alongside communicating and training the changes in systems out, we also applied sanctions for non-adherence – to show people how important this was. This carrot-and-stick approach has worked: the culture has changed – and I can sleep easier now!

- ***Multi-Skilling 'One Team Members'*** – in this industry, job demarcations for FOH staff are fast disappearing. The old days where staff members identified themselves by 'department' (reception, F&B, concierge, etc.) have long gone. Before I arrived, the company had attempted to impose a 'One Team Member' approach, where FOH staff were expected to multi-task according to the needs of customers at any given time. But it failed miserably because it wasn't obvious to the team why they should do it. What was in it for them? Staff turnover rose to 160%; disengagement was high. Something needed to be done. Working with the new HR Manager, we knew we had to start again. We wrote a suite of training manuals that would give staff the skills to complete tasks in different areas of operation. Also – crucially – we introduced a points-based 'grades of pay' system which rewarded staff (on a scale of 1–4) based on the skills they had acquired and the number of tasks they could perform. Resistance to the 'One Team Member' initiative crumbled; the disaffected all departed. Advocates and adopters took their places, and we have been able to grow a far more loyal and stable team (turnover is now beneath industry averages). Also, because we now have more multi-skilled staff, we need less labour; employment costs have declined as productivity has shot up.

These two change initiatives have been successful – but for different reasons. We were able to tighten up safety through a systemised approach, backed up with communications and sanctions. Multi-skilling was successful because we incentivised a change in behaviour. Successful outcomes, achieved through different means, to embed a more *agile, responsive change culture.*

# #8 MARKET AND CUSTOMER ANALYSIS

The eight ranked competency required for outstanding OD practice is Market and Customer Analysis. This is the ability to interpret and act on an accurate analysis of customer needs, feelings and aspirations, combined with deep insight into market trends and competitive behaviour. The qualities required for this competency include curiosity, social awareness and perceptual acuity, allied to analytical, processing and thinking skills[13].

---

13  For wider reading on leadership and customer intimacy, see 'Coaching Leaders to Ignite Customers' in Edger, C., and Heffernan, N., *Advanced Leader Coaching – Accelerating Personal, Interpersonal and Business Growth* (Oxford: Libri, 2020), pp. 124–41.

Again (like Planning and Organisation above), this competency is ranked lowly not because of its unimportance per se; rather, many of the respondents viewed this as an activity that was carried out by expert marketeers, negating the need for OD excellence in this facet of the role. However, it makes it to the roster of nine competencies because it has a vital link with Strategic Thinking (ranked third) and the fact that:

> Outstanding higher-order thinking ODs are really good at this, making a serious contribution at the strategic level through their Market and Customer analysis insights. But an important distinction is that the best – rather than just bringing day-to-day customer feedback to the table – tend to bring micro-insights that might have macro-impacts. Where do they shape these? By reading internal marketing reports, obviously – but also by being out of the office on the ground, ritually reading sector publications and connecting with their industry-side peer group…
>
> David Singleton, ex-Regional Vice President, Hard Rock Cafe

The issues that ODs face, both developing and exploiting this competency, include a lack of time, a deficit in intellectual horsepower and the fact that it is often too difficult to see the wood for the trees – on customers, markets and trends – given the voluminous and often contradictory information that confronts them. In order to boil it all down and get things straight in their own mind, however, outstanding ODs are great at directly listening to customers, tracking competitive behaviour and refreshing their industry knowledge through reading and networking. These will now be considered in turn.

## LISTENS TO CUSTOMERS

In this fast-moving age of super analytics, big data and AI, the OD will be presented with a truckload of information on their customers and market trends. In the past, ODs would have relied on Mystery Customer and NPS as their main sources of insight in this area – tools that have been superseded by analytics and algorithms combining real-time, 'spontaneous' digital and social-media customer data. While debates rage over its utility and efficacy (i.e. is it representative or corrupted?), there is little doubt that companies have become obsessed with driving customer advocacy through 'likes', 'meme shares', 'Google ratings', 'site clicks' and so forth. During COVID, however, market and customer analysis became more raw and faster moving for ODs:

> Situations change the priorities for ODs. During the COVID-19 pandemic, the focus on market and customer analysis and creative thinking has leapt to the fore – 'how can we keep our businesses going in the safest possible way?' led every conversation. It then moved into the more strategic longer term: 'what will the world look like post COVID?', 'what do we do as a company to come out of this bigger better and stronger?' But always in the continuous loop – 'what is changing?' Gelato flavours that hadn't been selling and indeed were due for delist shot to being the biggest sellers in the new world of delivery – as people's habits changed faster than at any other time in this millennium. A good OD is aware of these pivots in preferences, reviews them and makes 'speed to market decisions' with their team, to ensure that where opportunity exists, it's taken. But making the right strategic decisions will only generate success if you take the team on the journey with you, checking if they want to race down the path you are running down too.
>
> Elton Gray, Commercial and Operations Director, Creams Café

Clearly, seismic events such as COVID had an immediate effect on consumer behaviour (see Chapter One). The capacity of ODs to react and adapt their offers and service systems quickly during the crisis (truncating menus, extending service/delivery channels, incorporating digital order/pay apps) was proof of their ability to quickly react to consumer needs and trends. In more benign times, however, where behavioural change and trends move more slowly, the outstanding OD steals a march on their peers by:

- **Avoiding Cack Wizards** – rather than placing total reliance on so-called 'market experts' (who are generally totally detached from the actual customer), outstanding ODs will triangulate customer data from a number of sources to validate their hunches and insights.

- **Sophisticated Interpretation** – it is tempting and fashionable to swallow everything the customer tells us as being totally honest and factual. But erroneous opinion polling in developed Western economies recently (failing to predict the Brexit result and Trump's election win in 2016, and the Boris landslide of 2019) has demonstrated that people aren't entirely honest about disclosing what they really feel. Hence, in value brands, customers might complain about service but – in reality – the main driver of their absolute levels of satisfaction is price. In premium brands, consumers say they want quality (which they clearly do) but what they really crave is an experience that matches their perceived social standing and identity. Outstanding ODs read behind what customers are saying to understand what they actually feel and mean.

- **Understanding Breakpoints/Sensitivities** – this level of sophisticated interpretation of what their core consumers want helps outstanding ODs grasp what the key breakpoints and sensitivities in their proposition might be. That is to say – through close observation and sophisticated analysis – they know which element of the experience matters *most* to their customers (price, comfort, atmosphere, speed, quality, range, etc.) and are sensitive to the dire consequences of dialling down any element that is highly prized by the majority of their clientele.

### CASE STUDY 26 – GRASSROOTS LISTENING

*Elaine Kennedy is an Operations Director for Hawthorn (The Community Pub Company) covering the northern half of the UK (circa 200 leases/ tenancies, one Operations Manager and six BDMs). Previously, Elaine was a senior field operator for Punch and Greene King and was a 2018 graduate of BCU's MSc in Multi-Unit Leadership and Strategy (with distinction).*

Our business model is B-C-C (business to customer to consumer). Our tenanted/leased customers are distinct, if not mutually exclusive, from our community pub consumers. Why is reaching out and listening to both important? Firstly, our *tenanted/lessee customers*: they have to be listened to and engaged with because *they are our business*. Happy lessees = happy consumers = successful business partnerships! Also, it is important to listen to them because we can learn things from them and apply ideas more broadly across the estate. They are the experts in running wet-led community businesses and they are our *fonts of local knowledge* regarding micro-trends, needs and competitive threats. Secondly, our *pubs' consumers*:

they have to be listened to, especially in such a ferocious value-led market. We need to know how they behave and what they respond best to. Often, businesses can waste their resources spending money, time and effort on things that don't matter that much to the consumer. We have to carefully judge what their key sensitivities and breakpoints are. For instance – in our segment of the market – overspending on amenity and signage, when what our customers *really* want is an acceptable level of *comfort* and EDLP (every-day low pricing).

How do I listen to our tenants and lessees? In person! Nothing beats face-to-face, where you engage in some serious relationship building. Also, as an OD, you must go to sites where big decisions need to be made: capex investment calls or pivotal lessee recruitment decisions. To do this, I have to *protect my time* by limiting the number of meetings I have at Head Office; I've never been one to just 'show my face' for the sake of it, anyway. Sometimes, if I've got a gap in my day, I'll pop out with one of my BDMs and slot into their visits to show support and (more importantly) gather vital intelligence from the ground. Other mechanisms which we use to listen to our tenants/lessees include more formal mechanisms: surveys, WhatsApp forums, etc. But in my view, face-to-face remains the best way to keep connected with the real issues.

How do I listen to our pubs' consumers? If I get new units, have capex programmes scheduled or we need to change the offer somewhere, I spend time with the BDM – or on my own – at *grass-roots level*, visiting the area (having a cuppa in a local café, picking up the vibes by asking *'What pubs do you use? Which ones are the best? Why?'*). I also use social media – particularly Facebook – to find out what's going on in local towns and areas that accommodate our pubs. By joining local town Facebook groups, I can establish what people are taking about: which pubs they like, what the community issues are, what local charities they support and so forth. I've found this extremely useful when I turn up at our pubs: I can throw some local information into the conversation – it shows interest, helping to develop relationships.

What is good and bad OD practice in this area?

- **Detachment** – the worst ODs don't spend much time out in trade and become totally detached from their customers and consumers. The only time they seem to visit individual sites is when things become 'legal' and they have to be there! Why? Two reasons. First, many poor ODs like to slither around Head Office in order to raise their profile and burnish their credentials as the next MD. Second, many ODs in our industry have historically been middle-aged, middle-class men who just don't get – or want to get – our target market. They feel uncomfortable visiting community wet-led pubs because they feel out of place and ill at ease.

- **Grassroots Listening** – outstanding ODs, however, pursue a grassroots listening strategy. They get close by being visible, available, curious and authentic. They are known for building relationships (particularly with key opinion-forming tenants/lessees) – not because they are a pushover but because, when they say 'yes' or 'no', they mean it. They always deliver on promises and get back to people, one way or another, whether it is with good or bad news. They gain a reputation for being accessible, straight and honest.

In summary, outstanding ODs invest considerable *emotional energy* in listening to, and creating great relationships with, their customers in leased and tenanted businesses. They also get close to their consumers by being 'out there': watching, assimilating and processing behaviours. It can be exhausting and demanding – how do they keep going? Simple. Speaking for myself, you draw enormous energy from the *wins and successes* you have with your business partners. The *pride* you derive from listening and helping people succeed in this industry, more than compensates for the 24/7 effort you have put in to make it all work!

## TRACKS COMPETITORS

One of the most efficient ways of conducting market and customer analysis is to track what one's competitors are doing (successfully) and then quickly imitate them. Eliminating the search costs of design, pilot and trial in one fell swoop through fast and better followership is certainly one of the hallmarks of outstanding Operations Directors. Outstanding ODs will absorb what their competitors are doing through:

Extensive competitor visits and sampling. Outstanding ODs will make it their business to 'do the circuit' in their key trading areas during peak occasions to closely observe what works for customers and then go back to base and reverse engineer it into their businesses. Look at the industry over the past ten years and see how trends like sourdough pizza and cocktails were started off in one part of the industry and were then copied by everyone else. Another smart thing that outstanding ODs do is debrief newbies from their competitors to understand what worked in their 'operational black box' and what they could add to their new surroundings.

Alex Ford, Managing Director, Oakman Inns

However, outstanding ODs are quite discriminating on what they learn and take on board from competitors. Some innovations will not suit their customers or business model. Also, observing what their competitors try and fail to land can be just as informative as discovering what novel approaches or products they add value to their businesses with. In order to get under the bonnet of competitor businesses and learn about emergent trends, outstanding ODs will:

- **Leverage Peer Network** – most ODs will have worked in other businesses or have strong relationships with ex-colleagues who will be scattered around the industry. Utilising this network, they pick up on competitive innovation that will add manifest value to their business.

- **Related Industry Analysis** – in addition, observing company innovation in other, related service sectors will give outstanding ODs some inspiration for ideas that might work in their businesses (particularly with regards to digital and technology).

- **International Trend Analysis** – it was once said in hospitality that 'what the US did first, the UK did second'. This caricatured account was probably more accurate in the 1990s and 2000s (exemplified by the explosion in full-service casual, branded fast food and take-aways) but still carries an element of truth today. Studying what taste, product and technological trends are taking hold in the US, particularly, gives ODs some pointers as to what might be heading their way in the future.

## CASE STUDY 27 – CREATING COMPETITIVE ENVY

*Barrie Robinson is the National Operations Director and Board Director for Parkdean Resorts, the UK's largest holiday-park operator (with 67 sites, 22,000 owners and 440,000 holidaymakers per annum). A graduate of BCU's MSc in Multi-Unit Leadership and Strategy Programme (with distinction), Barrie was crowned ALMR BDM of the year (whilst at Greene King) in 2013.*

My role – and that of my field team (nine Regional Directors, 67 Resort Managers and the wider resort teams) – is to ensure that we create maximum value and enjoyment for the 22,000 owners of our resort pitches and the many guests that join us for a holiday break throughout the year. In order to do this, we need to do two things particularly well. First, stay ahead of the competition. Second, embrace our owner and holidaymaker feedback to make sure their experiences on the resorts are truly amazing and hassle-free. I will deal with both in turn.

First, how do I and my team ensure we stay ahead of our competitors?

- **Carve a Niche** – what we ask ourselves two or three times a year is what are we doing differently or not doing differently in comparison to our competitors? It is this differentiation that is key. By looking through all of their brochures, websites and public information, have we differentiated ourselves sufficiently? Have we found a niche? Can we own it? Does it give us clear competitive advantage?

- **Create Envy** – because what we are really trying to do is maintain our position as the most admired and crave-able proposition in the holiday resort sector. We want to be envied by our competitors! So, having looked 'narrow' by assessing our direct competitive set, we then go 'broad'. We look at consumer offers in sister segments of the market (say Centre Parks, YHA, Outward Bound) and ask ourselves: what can we learn? What can we steal with pride? In our case, we have recently extended our offer in four parks by opening up Activity Hubs offering pottery workshops, high tree walking, kayaking, zorbing, etc. This opens up our proposition to the wider 'active' leisure market and sets us apart from our direct competitive set.

- **Keep Learning** – but I insist that my team and I keep on top of our competitor analysis – constantly learning, comparing and (where necessary) incorporating best-practice insights. How? Through multiple means:

  - **Scraping their Websites** – constantly scrutinising competitor Tripadvisor and social-media sites to steal intelligence from their customer feedback.

  - **Mystery Customer Shops** – engaging neutral agencies to assess the quality of our competitors' product experience.

  - **Holidaying with Competitors Ourselves** – I go with my wife and family to competitor offers for a weekend, as do my Regional Directors. If nothing else, it prevents arrogance and complacency – because many of the experiences are outstanding!

  - **Local Price/Product Surveys** – we assess the direct and indirect amenity competition (pubs, holiday cottages, shops, etc.) within a mile-and-a-half and a fifteen-mile radius quarterly. How does our marketing mix stack up? Are we priced too high or low? Do we need to extend our premium or value offering?

  - **Interview Competitor Recruits** – this industry is a little village, really – people move around. When somebody joins us from a competitor, we ask them 'What were the best three things about your previous company?' Three weeks later, we ask them 'What are the biggest three opportunities we have to align ourselves or exceed your previous company?'

Whilst tracking competitors' behaviour and outstripping their offer is vital, so too is listening to customers. It is my passionate belief as an OD that, rather than being defensive or evasive about negative feedback, we should embrace it as an *opportunity*. To that extent, I have purposely driven a more *customer-centric culture* over the last couple of years by:

- **Strengthening Insight Loops** – every quarter, we hold owner forums which are attended by me, the Regional Director and GMs. This is structured on a two-way agenda basis: we update our owners on what we are investing in the resorts, listen to wider owner concerns and pick up on any opportunities that they suggest to us. The key messages we are trying to get over here are that we want to increase the 'lifetime experience value' and 'total service value' for owners. Also, monthly, our GMs hold drop-in sessions where owners can talk to us on a more personal level. All of this information is built into a tight insight loop which we treat as key, actionable information to improve our owner experience.

- **Reframing Customer Feedback** – when I took over as Ops Director, I made it quite clear that I didn't regard complaints as a threat, but rather as a 'registering of customer opportunity'. As cheesy as that sounds, I meant it. Complaints are an opportunity to enhance the service and value for our owners and holiday makers, if we respond quickly and appropriately.

- **Speeding up Response Times** – to that end, we put in place a twenty-four-hour immediate response, recognising complaints, and following up with a resolution letter within three days. This doesn't mean we solve everything to everyone's satisfaction – but we are seen to listen and care more about what our customers are saying.

- **Showcasing the Value Added** – actions we have taken from suggestions and complaints are then showcased to our owners. We go back to them saying 'you told us to do this, fix this, etc. – we've done this, etc.!' And they're not just big things. In my view, tiny improvements can make a significant impact with our customers, being perceived as highly value-added.

So what has been the result of all the work we have done around competitor tracking, listening to our customers and improving the service culture in our resorts? Owner engagement has increased, our holidaymaker net promoter scores are up and the tenure spans of our owners have increased by two-and-a-half years (including more upgrades)!

# *REFRESHES KNOWLEDGE AND INSIGHT*

Many ODs can be quite parochial and adopt a closed mindset to developments in their industry. By contrast, outstanding ODs retain an open, flexible mindset to the world around them, feeding their knowledge base – as outlined above – through direct competitor tracking (through peer networks, competitor visits and sampling, etc.). The best constantly recharge their knowledge banks through:

> Reading daily online news briefings like Propel Info, the Morning Advertiser and research stuff that comes from CGA/Peach. They also attend conferences and forums to listen to speakers highlighting the recent developments in their industry... the breaks between sessions also give them a great chance to network. Great ODs are like meerkats (up on their hind legs scanning the horizon) – bad ones are like moles (buried underground in the dark on their own).
>
> Clive Chesser, CEO, Punch Pubs & Co

However, highly ambitious ODs with a thirst for knowledge and a mission to carve out a higher profile will volunteer to:

- **Join Industry Bodies** – those willing to sign up to sitting on subcommittees on industry trade bodies will – in addition to making some great contacts – learn a great deal about the political, competitive and consumer forces underpinning the industry.

- **Speak at Events** – given the increase in industry events, conferences and symposia over the past ten years (that are always on the lookout for speakers!), plenty of opportunities exist – with their company's blessing – for ODs to share their knowledge with other like-minded operators. The very act of committing to and then delivering these talks also has a profound effect on sharpening and refining the OD's critical-thinking faculties!

- **Continuous Learning** – in addition, outstanding ODs will often be voracious listeners to business podcasts and readers of the latest 'guru' books. Whilst they retain a healthy scepticism concerning their universal claims for success and applicability, doing this helps unearth nuggets that can be profitably used by them both personally and organisationally.

## CASE STUDY 28 – REFRESHING KNOWLEDGE AND KEEPING ON-TREND

*Alex Ford is the Managing Director of Oakman Inns (29 premium pub–restaurant units, six direct reports). Previously, he occupied senior field positions in other major pub companies and is a graduate of BCU's MSc in Multi-Unit Leadership and Strategy Programme.*

I am constantly refreshing and updating my knowledge. Why? Because the world moves so quickly and any business you are building (like Oakman, founded by Peter Borg-Neal in 2005) has to remain relevant and on-trend. To my mind, things are moving faster because generational timeframes and industry paradigm shifts are being 'crunched'. What do I mean by this? Customers and employees that were born in the 1990s are moving and changing habits far quicker than previous generations, due to technology. Also, the digital landscape is shifting so fast, it is causing speedier and more spectacular changes in the way in which businesses transact, compared to previous times (when the pace of change and innovation was far slower). So, the simple fact is this: you have to stay on point as a senior field leader; you've got to keep up-to-date with what is happening at your industry level and – just as importantly – keep abreast of what is emerging elsewhere. The simple fact is that pubs are not necessarily a 'lead sector'; you've got to tap into trends (especially AI and big data) that are occurring in other industries in order to understand what is going to impact consumer behaviour in our sector next.

How do I do this? Obviously, I evaluate consumer and competitive behaviour in our businesses and around the sector by visiting, watching and listening. But I gain important intelligence from wider sources including:

- **Conferences** that showcase leading-edge speakers and provide the ability to network in between sessions.

- **Award ceremonies** (which Oakman have featured heavily in over the last six years) where I can pick the brains of the innovators and 'best in class' operators within the industry.

- ***Industry e-papers***, newsletters and journals like Propel, Langton Capital, MCA, etc. that provide up-to-date daily and weekly information on sector developments.

- ***Podcasts*** and audio-books (from sources like Amazon's Audible) that I consume as I travel nearly 30,000 miles a year around our units (which equates to spending nearly 13 weeks in a car!).

What all these sources enable me to do is assemble a vast amount of information on what is in vogue, what might lie on the horizon and (crucially) what's fading in fashion. But it is important to apply a filter to all of these sources. What is trending might suit some businesses, but not Oakman. What do I mean by this? The *experiential dining* market trend is raging in London at present, with eating experiences being 'dialled up' with supplementary leisure options (darts, ping pong, bowling, crazy golf, axe throwing, etc.). Young urban professionals love it – this combination of dining and so-called *competitive leisure*. But would this work for Oakman with its large home counties premium pub estate? It might appeal to urban professionals who *fringe* Oakman's demographic, but extending our dining experience in these *particular* ways would undoubtedly damage Oakman in the eyes of its *core consumer*. However, what we can take from this experiential dining trend is maybe improving our outside garden drinking experience (with traditional pub games: quoits, horseshoe pitching, boules, etc.) or exploiting some of our hotel cellar spaces (with 'Escape Room'-type dungeons) as really neat ways of sweating our assets.

In terms of things that I have learnt about and incorporated from my reading and networking, two things spring to mind:

- ***Urban Coffee trend*** – at Oakman, we are always looking at how we can exploit quieter 'shoulder' *timeslots* more effectively and increase *dwell times*. I heard about an artisan coffee operator in London that had really nailed 'taste and presentation' for the premium London market. We went with the same concept – recreating an up-market artisan experience (with the crockery etc.) – and it increased our traffic amongst business users and dwell times amongst habitual customers. One insight I gained from this, though, was that although the whole concept was right for us, I should have done more research on taste; we eventually dialled down the bitterness of the product after feedback from our customers!

- *Fine Wine trend* – there is a hell of a lot of ubiquity and convergence between wine lists in this industry. I picked up on what another small operator was doing with his wine lists in his units around Hampstead and studied them. It was clear that we were being too formulaic; this operator was receiving rave reviews for the variety and affordability of his selections. Again, we've learnt from this and are currently revamping our wine lists to get ahead of the pack once more.

So in summary, I would say that listening to and following the experts (as long as you apply a filter appropriate to your business) is an absolute must. My view is that the best Operations Directors have – in addition to relatively high levels of EQ and IQ – great levels of learning agility. Their businesses don't stand still because they are always learning and on the lookout for new trends and ideas that they can exploit to grow their revenue lines.

# #9 CREATIVE THINKING

The competency ranked ninth for outstanding OD practice was Creative Thinking, the ability either independently or collectively to facilitate original thinking outside the box that adds value to a business. ODs who practise and/ or encourage it recognise the virtues of bringing new perspectives or unorthodox solutions to bear in the pursuance of growing sales, cutting costs or increasing productivity. The skills and qualities required for this competency are lateral thinking, originality, risk-taking, imagination, open-mindedness and nurturing[14].

Linked to the previous competency – Market and Customer Analysis – it conceives of outstanding ODs as curious investigators of new ways of doing business (although this particular competency takes more of an *internal* rather than *external* perspective to idea generation). Its ranking at the bottom of the

14  For wider reading on leadership and creativity, see 'Coaching Leaders to Drive Innovation' in Edger, C., and Heffernan, N., *Advanced Leader Coaching – Accelerating Personal, Interpersonal and Business Growth* (Oxford: Libri, 2020), pp. 209–26.

OD competency table shouldn't invalidate its importance:

> Some of the best ODs I have come across are incredibly innovative and creative; either in a personal sense or in the way they encourage members of their team to experiment. It is often said that a lot of the great ideas in organisations come from the people that actually do the job. In Stonegate – by its nature an entrepreneurial organisation – we actively capture ideas at unit and area level and then exploit them across the company. For instance, many of our innovations around sports events (pre-ordering, table service, servers in identifiable shirts, stadium seating, key menu items) have either come from or been 'continuously improved' upon by our teams. We are always seeking to improve our marginal advantage – always on the lookout for any 'sparks' that accelerate sales!
>
> Colin Hawkins, Divisional Operations Director, Stonegate
> Group

Poor ODs would arrogantly dismiss the worth of encouraging bottom-up innovation or a *continuous improvement culture* because they regard it as their infallible right to come up with all of the best ideas. Either that or they brazenly steal the ideas that bubble up to claim them as their own! By contrast, outstanding ODs foster a climate of innovation by *empowering their people to think creatively, encourage inter-region/brand knowledge transfer* and stay alert to *evolve their offer and operations*. These will now be considered in turn.


## *EMPOWERS INNOVATION*

It is a powerful basic human instinct to seek some degree of autonomy and self-expression – societies and organisations that ignore this elemental truth do so at their own peril. It is therefore the job of the OD to harness this motivational need by empowering their team to experiment and seek out faster and better ways of doing things.

The best ODs give their people permission to fail. What do I mean by this? They create a trust-based culture where people feel comfortable trying things without fear of retribution if things go wrong. Clearly, we aren't talking about anarchy here! There will be rules and boundaries – but in general, ODs that outperform their peers cheerlead idea generation, recognising that it not only serves to increase engagement but can also add value to their business. I would say this OD behaviour, however, is more prevalent in smaller companies, where ODs are closer to the action and there is less bureaucracy, with faster decision-making processes…

Alex Ford, Managing Director, Oakman Inns

Outstanding ODs are in the business of being on constant lookout for micro-innovations in units and areas which they can harness across their region/brand. They will also set aside some time in their region/brand meetings with their AMs to harvest any insights and check on the progress of 'activated ideas'. As for themselves, creative overthinking is usually futile – instead, letting the unconscious mind work during periods of downtime enables the brain to exercise unconscious deliberation on the opportunities at hand. Moments of clarity and inspiration are rarely derived from sitting around a flip chart! In order to unleash the creative powers of their region/brand, outstanding ODs encourage:

- **'Disruption'** – the best ODs ignite creative juices throughout their team by chivvying their people to generate ideas that will give them a competitive edge. By framing creativity as a way of establishing and sustaining competitive advantage over their 'plodding rivals', they inject zeal and energy into their tribe.

- **Flexibility with a Fixed Frame** – nevertheless, they don't just permit unfettered, unregulated creativity that might blow up the business. People must nail the hygiene factors underpinning their businesses (standards, health and safety and procedural compliance) before they do the 'sexy' stuff!

- **Value-Added Deviance** – clever ODs also tap into their teams' visceral need to challenge Head Office heterogeneity by granting tacit approval for 'black ops' experimentation. The main rule here being that the ideas and initiatives that are trialled out of sight of Head Office must hold the prospect of adding manifest value to avoid accusations of mischief making and sabotage.

## CASE STUDY 29 – BOTTOM-UP INNOVATION

*Stephen Gould is the Managing Director of Everards (presiding over 170 pubs, a brewery and other commercial property interests with seven direct reports including three ODs – one brewing, one property and one pubs – and with five Business Relationship Managers). Previously, he held senior field positions within Bass Leisure, Bass Lease Company and Punch Taverns.*

In my view, the OD position is the *pivotal bridge* between central strategy and local implementation. Over the last sixteen years as MD at Everards, I have had three excellent pub ODs who have played a vital role in shaping strategy at an executive management level and then *interpreting, translating and communicating* it at field level – constantly checking back for understanding and implementation. Their fluency in *transporting* and landing strategy is vital to the organisation. But nobody in the business has a monopoly on good ideas – no company should assume that an OD can singularly drive growth and innovation, without listening and harvesting the best ideas from the front-line. A fine OD is one that has the self-confidence (inside certain parameters) to let go – not to lose control but to increase their influence! This sounds counterintuitive, but trusting your people and giving them the space to experiment and innovate increases the capacity of ODs to ask for more constancy of purpose in return. To my mind, therefore, the best ODs aren't control freaks; they are the *facilitators, coaches and catalysts for innovative cultures* and, in the process, increase their influence over their estate through buy-in and motivation.

But how have the ODs I have had working for me driven bottom-up creativity and innovation in the past?

- **Tenant to Business Owner!** – four years ago, we made a decision to change our description of 'tenants' to 'business owners'; our OD at the time was instrumental in this decision. The change in terminology was more than just symbolic – we were giving a respectful nod to the fact that our tenants had the courage to set up their own businesses in partnership with us. By their very nature, they are highly incentivised and naturally motivated to grow their businesses. They aren't inert tenants – 'semi-employees' of Everards – rather they are business owners who have risked everything to make a success of going it alone. By calling them 'business owners', we are changing mindsets amongst both parties (Everards and licensees): they are the people who should be creative and we are there to *cheerlead, facilitate and unlock their ideas*. Our OD at the time was determined that we shouldn't pretend we were operating a managed house business by proxy; rather, we should have the confidence and humility to be 'on receive' and provide fuel to our business owners' creative fire.

- *Digital Knowledge Sharing* – you might think that a company with a 171-year heritage might be averse to new technology, but we're not! Our senior field operators have been committed to using digital platforms as an enabler for sharing and communicating great ideas amongst our business owners for years. For instance, Everards has a closed Facebook page ('Everards Connect') in which we have built a *community* amongst our business owners. They conduct (mature) daily group conversations sparking ideas, innovation and creativity. It's uplifting and amazing, really; they are – on paper – competitors, but they are still willing to post and share what they have tried, what works and how. This self-regulating, intergroup conversation leapfrogs us and these spontaneous exchanges between business owners demonstrate to me and my OD that we are winning! The answer to driving better estate performance is no longer 'top-down' ODs telling people what to do, but real-time, on-trend knowledge sharing that can *instantly* move businesses forward.

- *Community Events* – in addition, we have a blended approach to communications, holding regular webinars, meetings and conferences where our business partners can swap ideas. In these forums, the OD is crucial: acting as a facilitator; they draw out ideas and insights from our business owners for cross-fertilisation across the portfolio. Approaching innovation with a community mindset – that you're not fully in control of the discussions and conversations, but merely the conduit for their transmission and sharing – takes guts; but it is the right thing to do!

Where have I seen ODs get it wrong or right, in terms of empowering creativity within family-owned regional pub businesses?

- *Heritage Mindsets* – over the years I've been in this job, in certain areas of the industry, I've seen operators grapple with the concept of trying to balance heritage with an innovation agenda. What do I mean by this? It is natural at times to believe that what has been done over the last 100 years can be replicated year in, year out. However, it is so important to show curiosity or humility, asking our community of stakeholders (tenants, customers, employees, local councils, etc.) what *they* could do to evolve their businesses. A strong freehold balance sheet can at times create a proprietorial mindset rather than building deep, trusting stakeholder relationships which fuel the future.

- *Customised Mindset* – an OD who worked with me for six years had previously worked for a regional brewer and then run his own business. When I interviewed him, I thought 'he's a bit different!' He had a real business-owner mindset. When he arrived at Everards, he said to me 'if you buy a Penguin book, it has a discreet logo that denotes quality, but the author and the content of the book determines whether it gets traction'. What he was saying was that he had looked at our estate festooned with Everards signage, which dumbed down the individual identity and personality of our pubs. From that moment, we reduced the Everards livery and signalling and amplified the differentiated propositions of each of our pubs: their business owners, its unique warmth, community offer, etc. Only someone who had been in the same position as our business owners could give us the real confidence to reduce our reliance on the badge and put our faith in ratcheting up the differentiated aspects of each our individual businesses. With extraordinarily effective outcomes!

So in order to get a family-owned regional pub company cooking on gas, you have to release people rather than constrain them, if you want to drive innovation. Trusting, community-orientated relationships founded on sociability and sharing build creativity – detached managerial decision-making doesn't! This takes time, effort and patience; but the best ODs are willing to do this – granting a fair degree of flexibility and autonomy, but getting far more back in return.

## *ENCOURAGES KNOWLEDGE SHARING*

Empowering people to think and act creatively is one dimension of OD practice in this area; another is the encouragement of knowledge sharing across the region/brand. Outstanding ODs recognise that – by their very nature – multi-site hospitality organisations, subdivided into areas, clusters and units, are highly competitive environments. The drive to be 'top dog' or an upper-quartile performer – for the acclaim and/or to avoid scrutiny or punishment – often results in selfish hoarding behaviours, where operators deliberately hide information and knowledge from one another in order to maintain competitive advantage. Indeed, outstanding ODs realise that they have cracked creativity and innovation in their region/brand when their people independently swap ideas and knowledge of their own volition:

> Nirvana is when you have created an environment where everyone helps one another out and spreads around good ideas – without you telling them to do it. That is a high-performing team. Obviously, technology like WhatsApp has been a great help here – someone can put out a question and 99% of the time one of the team will have an answer to the problem. Also, people who trial new ideas can post about their success, telling others and showing them, through pictures or short videos, how to do it!
>
> Jon Walters, Operations Director, Qbic Hotels

So outstanding Operations Directors clearly facilitate knowledge and information sharing within their region/brand, a process they can accelerate through:

- **Mobilising Channels** – actively sponsoring, supporting and getting involved in social-media channels that connect various cohorts (like Kitchen Managers, General and Assistant Managers, etc.) together for information-sharing purposes.
- **Increasing Bonding** – encouraging intermingling of various levels/cohorts of their region/brand at conferences, away days, and training and development sessions where sufficient attention is given over to social bonding and relationship building.
- **Rewarding Sharing** – publicly recognising and rewarding individuals in their region/brand who share value-added ideas to

underscore the contribution such behaviour makes to achieving a high-performance 'one-team' mentality.

---

## CASE STUDY 30 – FACILITATING KNOWLEDGE AND INSIGHT SHARING

*Scott Fowler is the Operations Director for the Eastern Division of Whitbread Restaurants (seven formats, 160 units and ten Retail Operations Managers). Previously, he held Regional Operations roles and Operations Manager roles in Brewers Fayre and Toby Restaurants. In 2014, he graduated from BCU's MSc Multi-Unit Leadership and Strategy Programme (with distinction).*

Getting my ROMs to swap knowledge and insights is relatively easy in Whitbread because, historically, the organisation has propagated a one-team culture. It is an organisation with a long and proud history, with long-serving employees with a great deal of pride in the company. Their preference is to share rather than hide. Having said that, ROMs are naturally competitive; I assist the process of knowledge and insight sharing in the following ways:

- **Set the Climate** – in order to prevent any kind of hoarding or selfish behaviour (keeping real value-added business ideas that have worked in certain districts to themselves), I purposely work upon creating a *culture of trust and reciprocity* amongst my ROMs. This is ultimately led by me – through the behaviours I display and reward. Don't get me wrong – it takes time. But getting everyone to understand that if 'they give, they will also receive' increases willingness amongst my ROMs to help one another; even when I don't ask them to!

- **Create Alignment** – but what tangible alignment mechanisms do I put in place to facilitate knowledge sharing?

  - **Overarching Goal and Vision** – the first thing you have got to do is build a collective desire to achieve something – together! Get people to understand that the common good transcends personal gain. To that end, my vision and goal is 'we want to be the best we can possibly be' and if we are, 'we will be the best division'.

- **Monthly Ops Meetings** – getting ROMs to think outside their districts and about the performance of the wider division is key. At monthly Ops Meetings, I actively encourage the sharing of best practice.

- **WhatsApp Groups and Microsoft Teams** – outside of formal channels, however, technology has been a great enabler for ROMs to set up their own groups, spontaneously connecting to ask questions and share ideas.

- **Bonding Events** – also, events such as conferences and away days enables my ROMs to bond on a deeper level, getting to know one another as people – building up respect, trust and understanding. After all, some of the best ideas are exchanged over a beer rather than over a meeting table.

But whilst this is all worthy – where's the money in this? I've got two examples where initiatives that were proposed and driven by my ROMs have added real value;

- *Local Marketing Portal* – like all large branded organisa-tions, local field operators often rely (too much) on Central Marketing to drive traffic, promotions and sales. But often these 'global' initiatives are not fit for local micro-market purposes. Local customisation is sometimes essential – even in national brands – to unlock value! My ROMs came up with the ideas on this, working together; they designed a sweep of tools for a 'Local Marketing Portal' and empowered their GMs to access for tactical 'market share grabs'. The result? A real spike in sales performance that the ROMs and GMs had owned and sustained themselves.

- *Premier Inn Breakfasts* – obviously many of our sites are co-located with our sister Premier Inn hotel brand. What came through on customer feedback was that our breakfast provi-sion was falling somewhat short on quality and speed. In my Division two ROMs took up the reigns on this, co-opted Regional champions and devised a training programme (based on best practice they harvested from around the Region). Ways of working for GMs and DMs were also adjusted; administration duties were shifted to non-peak periods so that they could lead the line on the floor during breakfast sessions.

> The result? Satisfaction turned bright green on the scorecard and Premier Inn were able to (justifiably) charge more on the room rate!

On a personal level, as well, it is important that I share my knowledge and insights at a strategic level within the organisation. In addition to my OD field role, I have a matrix responsibility for 'value formats' across Whitbread. This has given me the opportunity to sit on Steering Groups evolving our current formats, whilst inventing, trialling and rolling out new ones. I've spent my career in brands that have served blue-collar workers, young families and value-seeking silver surfers. To that end, I am able to bring my philosophy and mantra relating to this segment of the market (namely: 'stay in your lane') to debates around value-brand development. All too often, I have seen value brands drift away from their original core purpose; their DNA is diluted, their founding mission forgotten and their noble brand archaeology dismissed by over-enthusiastic 'marketing engineers' who may not naturally empathise and connect with this demographic. I like to think my role is one of bringing people 'back to centre' on what value customers really crave and what really animates them. Competency levels are different in this market – customers respond to different signalling. That is the knowledge and insight I bring to the party!

## EVOLVES FORMAT

Empowering creativity and facilitating knowledge sharing will come to nothing unless the OD standardises and incorporates the best ideas *across* their operations, thereby incrementally evolving their entire format. Too often in multi-site hospitality, ODs might be good at encouraging ideas and getting people to share but they are poor at gaining scalable advantage from them because:

> One of the reasons Creative Thinking is at the bottom of the competency ranking is because, in the chaotic, resource-starved world of multi-site operations, average ODs just strive to keep their heads above water! Time for creativity is a luxury, when survival is the main thing on their minds. However,

COVID has changed a lot of this. This cataclysmic event has served as a burning platform, proving to operators that they can jog and chew gum – run operations whilst rethinking and then quickly implementing a 'new normal' for staff and customers. Post-COVID, the imagination and speed-to-market that ODs have displayed across the industry over the past twelve months should be a bonus to their companies in years to come!

Steve Worrall, Managing Director, St Austell Pubs, Inns & Hotels

In order to capture, test and roll-out the best ideas – ensuring that their benefits are embedded across the portfolio – outstanding ODs:

- **Enlist Advocates** – build a guiding team of evangelists who – having established proof of concept – act as its advocates across the region/brand.

- **Violently Implement** – in multi-site hospitality, some of the best ideas bite the dust due to a lack of project management and implementation skills. A properly resourced, well-co-ordinated plan needs to be put in place – with sufficient monitoring and checkpoints – to ensure a successful roll-out. In addition, embedding new ideas (i.e. ways of working, revised product offerings or service delivery mechanisms) in the region/brand's operational blueprint will further strengthen sustainability.

- **Exercise Ambidexterity** – however, sometimes the ideas or changes will only apply to a select number of units (due to demographics or unit size) within the OD's portfolio; particularly in unbranded and L&T estates. Therefore, the *right* units must be tagged and targeted for improvement with the rest retaining business-as-usual offers and systems. Running different tiered offers, with differing speeds of evolution in unbranded and L&T portfolios, requires extreme ambidexterity on the part of outstanding ODs.

## CASE STUDY 31 – BOTTOM-UP EVOLUTION

*Ric Fyfe is the Operations Director (Scotland and Northern Ireland) for Gather & Gather, an artisan contract catering company owned by Mitie. He is responsible for 80 contract units, with six Regional Manager direct reports. A thirty-plus-year senior field hospitality veteran (which included a stint at Planet Hollywood), Ric graduated from BCU's MSc in Multi-Unit Leadership and Strategy Programme (with distinction) in 2013.*

Companies that think that they can just impose top-down innovation upon hospitality brands are mistaken – you can't just 'whitewash' a business from a distance. If you want to constantly tweak and evolve brands, you have to listen to and engage with employees and customers at the front end of the business. For sure, there will be times when change is derived from external paradigm shifts – such as social media, AI and the digitalisation of operations – but, fundamentally, the consumer-facing proposition can only be successfully evolved in *learning cultures* where intelligence is gathered from the front-line. This is particularly important in a contract catering business such as Gather & Gather, where we seek to differentiate ourselves not just on price (like so many other companies operating in this cut-throat space) but through our commitment to offering quality artisan food and drink, combined with truly exceptional service in the 'last three feet'. If we are to maintain these points of differentiation, we have to be alert to what the feelings, wants and needs of our customers are at any given time, to ensure the brand remains fresh and contemporary.

But how do I capture the best ideas from the front-line and my direct team, in order to drive this business forwards?

• **Climate of Trust** – the first thing I did when I arrived six years ago was change the culture of my team from being frightened and afraid to being *trusting, confident and proactive*. I made a number of decisions early doors that resolved many of the issues that had been derailing my team up to that point; and – to show them that I had *integrity* – I stuck with those decisions! Behaviour breeds behaviour, and soon my Regional Managers were adopting the same *empowering* managerial styles with their GMs, unlocking creativity and ideas where it mattered most – at the *moment-of-truth points* during encounters with the customers.

- **Personal Visibility** – in order to decrease the *geographical and psychological distance* between myself and the units, I have purposely spent 80% of my time in our contract restaurants and coffee bars – plugging in my laptop or getting behind the counter to increase my visibility and connectivity with my teams. What this has meant is that – over time – my GMs and teams were no longer scared of me; I became part of the furniture. As they relaxed, they found that they could have *honest, direct, trusting conversations*, telling me what we should stop, start or continue doing in order to grow our performance. I could filter this and act immediately on things that would add demonstrable value.

- **Digital Knowledge Sharing** – over the past few years, our teams have set up *WhatsApp groups* (chef, barista, GM, etc.) where ideas have been spontaneously shared and positives have been *communally celebrated*. Distinctive *communities of practice* have grown, where people with common skills, passions and aspirations can help one another advance and improve both personally and business-wise. In my view, this also substantially contributes to better *well-being*, as our people – in dispersed multi-unit contexts – no longer feel they are alone in feeling and thinking the way they do. It helps give them perspective and support.

- **Cross-fertilisation** – at Regional Manager level, I encourage cross-fertilisation of ideas in two main ways. First, through monthly *operational meetings* (which are split off from the financial review meetings), which are always held at one of our units. Each RM is tasked with bringing something new they've trialled that will add value to the business or things that they have learnt when they have *'caught someone doing it right'*. We also take time to sympathetically appraise and evaluate the particular business at which we are holding the meeting: 'what are the standards like?', 'how hassle free is the customer journey?', 'how does our offer fit with customer needs, wants and expectations?' Second – and this is critical – I always hold a *Friday afternoon 'catch up'* with my team, to review the week and talk about the weekend. It is essentially a social, 'problem-free' call where we can cheer one another on – making people feel good about themselves – so that they can hit the following week with a positive frame of mind. It also builds team *relationships and bonding*, resulting in my people actively wanting to help one another – *swapping resources and ideas* – rather than selfishly hiding or hoarding them.

By giving people the opportunity to have some input and control over their work environment, you unlock huge amounts of discretionary effort and creativity, which nudges and evolves our product, processes, people development, promotions, etc. But at the same time, my people have to earn the *ticket to play*, namely: their standards and health and safety operating procedures have to be exemplary. For my own part – as an OD – I can never be seen to be 'walking by' lapses in quality because it will be taken as *tacit approval*, leading to habitually poor practices. In the small number of cases where 'brains have been taken over by aliens', we have to take swift, corrective action. But, in the main, if you get the culture right, keep close to the units and show you care about your people, you can really incrementally improve the business from the bottom up!

# BRIEF SUMMARY

This chapter has – as a consequence of the empirical research and case studies derived from the twenty-seven respondents – outlined the *role, competencies and practices* of outstanding ODs. As such, it contains a treasure trove of insights and deep reflection from the respondents that will greatly assist aspirant ODs and their developers[15]. But – standing back – what are we to make of it all?

First, the respondents believed that the OD *role* had an optimum span of control and portfolio size, contingent upon its various business-model guises (managed unbranded, single-branded, multi-branded, L&T and franchised), beyond which executing its duties and responsibilities effectively was rendered virtually impossible. Second, the role was characterised by 'stylistic nuances' according to business model typologies: unbranded managed required ODs with a *'streetfighter mentality'*; single-branded managed, *'monomaniacal'*; multi-branded managed, *'chameleon'*; L&T, *'negotiator'*; and franchised, *'policeman'*. Third, in spite of these differing 'centres of gravity', the twenty-seven interviewees agreed that generic commonalities prevailed

---

15 Turn to the Conclusion for an integrated OOD Model and Framework that provides a 'one-stop' reference and checklist of the competencies, practices and qualities highlighted in this chapter.

among outstanding OD *competencies and practices*. They agreed that the top three outstanding OD competencies – given the *'people centricity'* of both the industry and role – were *cultural and behavioural*: 'Leading to Win', 'Building Capability' and 'Influencing and Alliance Building'. These were closely followed by a *cognitive thinking* cluster of competencies ('Strategic Thinking', 'Commercial Nous' and 'Profit Impact') which enabled ODs to optimise the exacting *commercial* requirements of the position. The final three – 'Planning and Organisation', 'Market and Customer Analysis' and 'Creative Thinking' – although deemed important, were either seen (certainly in the case of the first) as hygiene factors or (in the latter two cases) as activities that could be discharged more effectively elsewhere.

Furthermore, the case studies provided by the respondents – illuminating the main practices that underpin each competency – provide a wealth of detail relating to how outstanding ODs bring these vital competencies alive! Remarkably, there is one binding insight that resonates throughout all of the twenty-nine case studies in this section, namely: that **outstanding ODs are adept at creating vibrant regional/brand cultures**! Adjectives and descriptors such as 'winning', 'people-centric', 'collaborative', 'progressive', 'meritocratic', 'learning', 'open', 'inclusive', 'empowering', 'challenging', 'honest', 'trusting', 'forward-looking', 'profit-focused', 'commercial', 'operationally excellent', 'agile', 'responsive', 'change-driven', 'continuous improvement' and 'customer-centric' preceded the word 'culture' in many of the case studies, underscoring both its importance and multi-faceted, nuanced nature. But what are the implications of this finding? Quite simply, that culture can be defined as 'the collective programming of the mind which distinguishes the members of one group from those of another'. Thus, outstanding ODs are adept at shaping the *collective software of their followers' minds* by espousing, modelling and driving a common vernacular and *ways of doing things around here*. Why? The best ones understand that building a positive, idiosyncratic, binding culture is their most effective weapon against their greatest enemy – geographical and psychological distance.

But all of this analysis now begs an obvious question. If this section has given us a better idea of the principal competencies and practices of outstanding ODs, how can they be developed or further enhanced in aspirant and/or existent ODs? It is to this question that this book will now turn.

## CHAPTER THREE

# OD CAPABILITY DEVELOPMENT

The previous chapter outlined the nature of the OD *role* (its optimum spans of control, portfolio sizes and differing business-model requirements), followed by an elucidation of the nine main *competencies* in rank order of importance, combined with accompanying key *practices* required to operate at a high level. With regards to competencies, the research revealed two significant findings:

- The top three rated competencies for ODs – Leading to Win, Building Capability, and Influencing and Alliance Building – are *cultural and behavioural* skills. The following six competencies – Strategic Thinking, Commercial Nous, Profit Impact, Planning and Organisation, Market and Customer Analysis, and Creative Thinking – are *cognitive thinking* and *technical skills*.

- Crucially, the top three ranked OD competencies (Leading to Win, Building Capability, and Influencing and Alliance Building) – along with Strategic Thinking – were perceived to constitute the biggest stretch from the AM role.

Clearly then, developers of ODs have to ensure that potential candidates for the role have the capability to 'step up' in these four important areas and apply the right development mechanisms accordingly. How? Currently, the identification of potential ODs and their concurrent development is done poorly in most multi-site hospitality organisations. Why? Firstly, generic rather than OD-role-specific competency assessments are used to evaluate suitability and capability, resulting in delayed performance or outright failure by appointees. Secondly, high-performing AMs – automatically assumed to have the 'right stuff' for the role – lack the 'rounded cultural, behavioural and cognitive capacity' to ascend to the OD level and are quickly found out after experiencing a huge jump up in responsibilities. Thirdly, in the absence of scientific rigour to assess potential, candidates are promoted due to 'myopic favouritism' rather than 'what they might be capable of achieving'.

Fortunately, the research for this book should give aspirant ODs and their developers a more empirically grounded approach to identifying, selecting and developing outstanding ODs. Also – in addition to rank-ordering outstanding OD core competencies and their key practices – the respondents were asked how OD *potential* was best assessed and which *development* interventions were most effective in nurturing outstanding performance in the role. These will be outlined in turn, followed by some illuminating findings regarding *frequently asked questions* relating to the role.

# IDENTIFYING POTENTIAL ODs

In order to establish how best to identify OD potential, I asked the twenty-seven senior respondents to pick the top three methods of internally identifying talent from the following eight mechanisms: consistently high AM/BDM performance, appraisals, assessment centres, fast-track schemes, coaching/mentoring programmes, deputy OD/senior AM performance, executive talent management discussions and senior sponsorship. Out of these eight, four were overwhelmingly selected as being the most important, namely: *deputy OD/senior AM performance, consistently high AM/BDM performance, coaching/mentoring* and *senior sponsorship.* Why? Each of these 'potential identifiers' confirmed the capability to do the role, correlating with the top competency requirements to do the job well:

- **Deputy OD/Senior AM Performance** – the prime competency requirement for outstanding ODs is *Leading to Win.* The respondents agreed that this could be spotted amongst some who assumed deputy OD/senior AM positions, demonstrating that they had *resilience*, confidence, heft and credibility to *lead their peer group.* Indeed, often these leadership qualities were demonstrated by AMs without any formal status:

  > You can spot potential ODs by tracking those who take an informal leadership role in your regional team… influencing and leading their BDM peers by acting maturely and optimistically – finding solutions rather than problems – putting their hands up to get things done.
  >
  > Elaine Kennedy, Operations Director, Hawthorn
  > (The Community Pub Company)

- **Consistently High AM/BDM Performance** – allied to this, respondents cited 'consistently high AM/BDM performance' as being a major signal of OD potential. Nonetheless, consistent P&L performance was taken as a given – what made potential ODs stand out was being *famous for something* that had added manifest value within the organisation, whether it was opening high-risk airport properties for Premier Inn (Jon Walters) or opening a £70k Wahaca site in Cardiff (Gavin Smith). Doing something famous rather than just doing the job well signalled an ability amongst the best AMs to step out of their comfort zone and – acting with *grit*, courage, energy and determination – to really bend the curve. Also, OD potential in AMs could be spotted not only through 'single acts of fame', but their ability (crucial in other highly ranked OD competencies, *Building Capability* and *Strategic Thinking*) to make their areas 'famous' for their *positive can-do cultures*, focused direction, collective energy, execution and delivery – the foundations for which were clarity and building exceptional talent, skills and stability:

> Potential ODs have usually built a succession of winning teams at AM level, through focus, clarity and investing in their people. Their areas become famous as hotbeds of talent and energy – and when they move on, their best people often try to follow them!
>
> Helen Charlesworth, Executive Managing Director, Stonegate Group

- **Senior Coaching/Mentoring and Sponsorship** – the other significant method of identifying OD potential internally was – having come to the fore by standing out amongst their peers – the *senior sponsorship* and *coaching and mentoring* of promising candidates. But what did respondents mean by picking these two mechanisms as a means of identifying OD talent? I have already alluded to the fact that favouritism is the enemy of outstanding performance. What the respondents meant by selecting these factors was that OD potential had to be registered, recognised and acknowledged by a number of executives in the organisation, so that *collective advocacy* catalysed their advancement. To this extent, aspirant AMs needed to demonstrate the qualities associated with the third ranked OD competency, *Influencing and Alliance Building*, by already being visible at executive and Head Office level. Not by slithering around the corridors currying favour, but through forming relationships during *coaching/mentoring sessions* or helping out on important central initiatives or working parties – in short, burnishing a reputation for soundness, maturity and collaboration at the centre:

The reason why a lot of good AMs don't make it to OD is because they have a strong aversion to Head Office and everything they think it stands for. Also, given the choice, they would run a million miles from senior executives; they hate the thought of managing upwards. They figure that performance alone will get them to the next level – but it won't! They have to raise their profile at the centre and develop a fan base. Independently asking an MD or senior executive for informal coaching or mentoring is a start... the very fact that they have taken the initiative to seek senior counsel is a strong indication that they really want to progress to OD level...

Vanessa Hall, ex-Chair and CEO, Vapiano S.E.

The four means of identifying potential that languished behind the mechanisms alluded to above were *appraisals, talent planning, fast-track schemes* and *assessment centres*. Why? As formal HR mechanisms, they failed to draw out and illuminate the top four critical competencies (Leading to Win, Building Capability, Influencing and Alliance Building, and Strategic Thinking) required for the role, which are also the greatest stretch from the AM role. As such – to reiterate – these were highlighted better through deputy OD/senior AM performance (i.e. leading their AM/BDM peers), consistently high AM/BDM performance (i.e. being famed for value-added acts and building can-do area cultures), senior sponsorship, and coaching and mentoring (i.e. building strong advocates).

## ACCELERATING OD DEVELOPMENT

Having identified potential ODs, how do developers prepare them to step up? To a certain extent, AMs/BDMs signposting potential have – as outlined above – done so by signalling their promise through: taking a leadership role amongst their peers, finding fame through the singular and collective efforts of their team, and being visible at the centre. However – in a more formal manner at least – what development mechanisms are *guaranteed* to propel AM/BDMs to high-performing OD status? In my interviews with respondents, I asked them to choose what they regarded as the 'top three development mechanisms that prepared Area Managers for the OD role' from the following: interim OD roles, strawberry-patch OD roles, working at the centre in a functional role, central project-management roles, executive education and senior mentoring/coaching. In rank order, the respondents believed the most effective OD development interventions were:

1. **Senior Mentoring/Coaching**[16] – ranked highest by the respondents as being the most successful OD development mechanism, senior mentoring/coaching from executives was regarded as the most effective accelerator because it:

   o Built relationships and networks at a senior level

   o Provided wisdom, tacit knowledge and a sounding board (on organisational complexity, *culture* and politics) from someone who had 'climbed the executive ladder'

   o Created alliances, advocates and supporters at the 'top table'

   o Provided role models whose positive *'cultural traits'*, values and approaches aspirant ODs could imitate

   o Increased mental toughness, conviction and confidence (particularly amongst female AM/BDMs).

> During my career, moving between different senior people in a mentoring and coaching capacity was absolutely key getting me to OD level; helping me with exposure, relationships and development…
>
> Gavin Smith, Managing Director, Pizza Pilgrims

2. **Executive Education** – ranked second (and possibly a surprise to some!), Executive Education was perceived by respondents to be the next significant OD development accelerator – particularly for non-graduate AMs/BDMs – because it:

   o Had a 'game-changing' effect on AM/BDM maturity, confidence, mindsets and paradigms

   o Enabled AM/BDMs to equip themselves with the vocabulary and writing skills to operate at a higher operational level

   o Increased AM/BDM critical thinking, evaluation, presentational and problem-solving skills

---

16  For specific reading and instruction on how to coach high performers and transitioning leaders, see Edger, C., and Tucker, M., *Coaching Senior Hires – Transitioning Potential into Performance Quickly!* (Oxford: Libri, 2019) and Edger, C., *Coaching Star Performers – Reframing Negative Feelings and Drivers* (Oxford: Libri, 2019).

o   Exposed AMs/BDMs to a more strategic and holistic perspective of high-performing *organisational cultures* and their key dependencies

o   Gave ambitious AM/BDMs a significant point of differentiation within their competitive set.

> My PGDip and MSc were a confidence booster and huge validation of my critical-thinking skills… it did prove a decisive factor in my promotion to OD. Executive education is particularly good for 'Cinderella people' who might have been overlooked and missed for OD. It gives them greater recognition and also lights a fire under them… they think 'I can do this!' Executive education fans the flames for good AMs – it supercharges them to want to get to the next level.
>
> Colin Hawkins, Divisional Operations Director, Stonegate Group

3.  **Strawberry-Patch OD Roles** – in addition to the interventions above which hone OD behavioural and cognitive competencies, giving high-potential AM/BDMs strawberry patches (i.e. NOT span-breakers but autonomous region/brands with *fewer AMs and a smaller portfolio size*) grew individuals into outstanding ODs by:

o   Affording them an opportunity, in a 'controlled environment', to build confidence and *resilience,* and the opportunity to experiment constructing a *'winning culture'*

o   Limiting the risk of terminal career failure through 'baby steps' progression

o   Providing a safe space in which to develop, polish and extend AM-to-OD 'stretch competencies'.

> The strawberry patch at Oakman was extremely helpful for me to ease into the role… crucially (from AM/BDM level), it helps you learn to adapt your leadership style and approach, as you become more detached and distant from front-line day-to-day operations. The GM-to-AM transition in this respect is difficult. But the AM-to-OD transition is even harder!
>
> Alex Ford, Managing Director, Oakman Inns

4. **Interim OD Roles** – ranked behind strawberry-patch roles, interim OD roles – due to their transitory, just 'filling in' nature – were the fourth ranked development intervention, helping to:

   o Give aspirant ODs a chance to make an impact and shine

   o Grant more direct exposure to senior levels

   o Act as a safer, less-pressurised proving ground.

> I did holiday reliefs for some of my ODs (looking after five other BDMs)… What it enabled me to do was get prepped for key meetings and calls as if I were the OD. I found them a real opportunity to demonstrate insight and impact. What you mustn't do is just sit back and 'fill in'. Embrace the opportunity and prove you are up to it!
>
> Mike O'Connor, Operations Director, Greene King Pub Partners

5. **Working at the Centre in a Functional Role** (seconded or permanent) – the fifth rated development intervention – working at the centre in a functional role – was ranked lower due to a perception that sticking AM/BDMs in Head Office jobs sometimes 'cancelled them' or made them disappear off the radar. Nevertheless, doing a central role (most typically in an operational excellence capacities) was regarded by some as being useful to:

   o Understand the *mentality/culture* of the centre (politics, agendas, timescales and pace: how you get things done around there!)

   o Build alliances, relationships and networks

   o Observe the critical interdependencies between the functions and internal/external stakeholders

   o Abandon field-vs-centre and insider-vs-outsider misconceptions

   o Develop techniques and approaches to create mutuality, reciprocation and indebtedness with key resource holders to create win–win outcomes.

> I did a Central Ops role… it was key to helping me understand that there is no 'them' and 'us'! Prior to that, I had fought the centre rather than worked with them. Also, you get to

understand the mentality of the centre in order to get things done. The centre has a 9–5 mindset, whereas the field has a 24/7 one. Hence, you've got to push them in a different way.

James Pavey, National Operations Director, Tesco Cafés

6. **Central Project Management Role** (seconded or permanent) – rather than taking up a substantive functional role, exposing potential ODs to the centre through project roles came bottom of the list. Why? It was still perceived as being useful by some respondents but not necessarily an accelerator for outstanding performance. That said, the benefits for ODs include:

   o Raising their profile and extending their networks

   o Bringing field-based insights to commercial challenges/ opportunities

   o Gaining an insight into Head Office *behaviour/culture*.

Central project roles and functional appointments/secondments can be disastrous for field operators who are used to managing their own time. If it goes well – great! If it goes badly, they risk going from hero to zero in full sight of the decision-makers! So, I'd say there is a median success rate with these roles and certainly the field operators that do them need air cover, back up and understanding from senior people…

Helen Charlesworth, Executive MD, Stonegate Group

# FAQs FOR OD DEVELOPERS

My line of enquiry into how potential ODs are spotted and then developed has hopefully yielded some interesting insights for the developers of ODs. What emerges is that both processes (identification and then developing) are intimately connected to calibrating and then bolstering the nine behavioural and cognitive competencies identified in the previous chapter. In particular, the major competency gaps between the AM and BDM roles (Leading to Win, Building Capability, Influencing and Alliance Building, and Strategic Thinking) can be addressed by applying the top three development mechanisms identified above, namely: *senior coaching/mentoring, executive education and strawberry OD patches* – with, perhaps, the first two interventions preceding an actual OD field appointment. Certainly, senior coaching/mentoring should be continued for newbie ODs running strawberry patches, to ameliorate the anxieties, fears and frustrations naturally involved with stepping up into such a highly pressured appointment.

Nonetheless, in addition to how one spots potential and develops ODs, other challenges, paradoxes and conundrums remain for developers that are worth exploring: why do so many companies opt for external OD appointments? Do lifer AMs make better ODs than lifer OD appointments? Why are so few female AMs appointed to OD positions? Do graduate ODs outperform non-graduates? What types of OD do businesses usually lack (entrepreneurs, scalers, evolvers or turnaround specialists)? Exploring interviewee responses to these frequently asked questions (FAQs) will furnish the developers of ODs with further insights into some of the nuances, contradictions and complexities of accelerating OD talent.

- **Why do so many companies opt for external OD appointments?** – as prosaic and logical as the top two sections in this chapter are on internally unearthing and developing high-performing ODs, the reality is this: most companies (especially smaller multi-site hospitality and regional family-owned ones) tend to go external when they appoint ODs. Why? It was the respondents' belief that companies go external due to:
  - **Unconscious Bias** – a familiarity with the baggage, weaknesses, 'warts' and shortcomings of internal candidates, which leads to negative unconscious bias against them in selection processes.
  - **Avoidance of Peer Conflict** – a recognition (particularly in smaller companies) that promoting AM/BDMs to manage their peers risks potential conflict and discontent.
  - **Lack of Development** – an acknowledgement (which this book is a major response to!) that they have risible and amateurish internal systems for OD identification, development and progression.
  - **Risk Reduction** – a perception that levels of operational risk will be reduced by going for external OD candidates that have got the 'sheriff's badge' (having had experience of scaling up, evolving or reviving operations).

o **Fresh Perspective** – a view that hiring externally will give the organisation fresher insights and perspectives through an injection of contemporaneous competitive/market knowledge.

o **Change Impact** – a belief that a 'new broom will sweep clean', implementing change more easily than 'group-think' internals.

o **Hoarding** – a selfish desire to maintain the status quo at Area Management level, keeping high performers in situ to defend the P&L; in addition, some companies have a perverse aversion to giving internals large pay rises.

So, is hiring externals a good thing? As outlined above, there are some legitimate reasons why it can be. Indeed, the reality is that – especially in large corporates – it is healthy and progressive to have a fusion of internal and external appointments at OD level. But recruiters need to be cognisant of the fact that transitioning ODs into organisations from outside is often beset with *cultural issues*, with new recruits often experiencing delayed performance or outright failure because of a lack of fit. Certainly, companies shouldn't fall into the trap of constantly going outside for quick fixes:

> I liken the appointment of ODs within food-service companies to football management. When things are tough, it is always tempting to plump externally for instant, instead of gradual, success, which promises immediate shareholder returns. In casual dining, ODs typically had two-year lifecycles: 'land, deliver or fail, move on!' The typical response to any problem being 'change the team!' Also, in pubs you see a merry-go-round and regurgitation of individuals across the industry. Not healthy… and it blocks talent.
>
> Elton Gray, Commercial and Operations Director, Creams Café

• **Do 'lifer' AMs make better ODs than 'lifer' functional appointments?** – another question that is often asked is whether it is better to recruit ODs purely from the line – or are talented functional experts capable of doing the role? There were four broad responses from the interviewees to this question:

- **Yes – lifer AM appointments are better because:**
  - They've accumulated deep tacit knowledge of *'field culture'* over the years
  - Having grown up in the field, they 'get' and understand the people – they are safer bets
  - They are more adept at leading at a distance (creating *'winning cultures'*)
  - They have greater credibility (due to their 'hard yards') with front-line operators.
- **No – lifer functional appointments are better because:**
  - If they stick at OD, they make better MDs and COOs
  - They have better critical reasoning and cognitive thinking skills
  - They are more effective at resolving issues through persuasion and bargaining rather than coercion.
- **Both line and functional experience is the best combination because:**
  - It gives ODs greater breadth and agility
  - It breaks the silo mentality of dyed-in-the-wool field operators
  - It builds an appreciation of the issues facing both the field and the centre
  - It helps alliance and relationship building both in the field and at the centre.
- **It doesn't matter as long as:**
  - They are great people managers and *culture builders* regardless of background!

In my view, it doesn't matter where you originate as an OD – the field, the functions or both. To me, it is quite simple: to be an outstanding OD, you need the magic of leadership and commercialism! It doesn't matter where you were 'born' from.

Helen Charlesworth, Executive MD, Stonegate Group

- **Why are so few female AMs appointed into OD positions?** – one of the main conundrums in the hospitality industry is why there are so few female senior field operators, given the fact that females account for over 50% of GMs in some organisations! It is also mystifying, given the relative outperformance of female ODs versus men:

> The lack of progression of females in this industry into OD roles is a crying shame because female ODs uphold better standards and discipline; they are more detail conscious than men, creating more *'professionally minded cultures'*. Also, crucially, they have better emotional intelligence and deal with trickier situations more honestly, directly and compassionately than men…
>
> Simon Longbottom, CEO, Stonegate Group

> 50% of my ODs at Punch are female – almost without exception, the females that rise through are better than men; they are more tenacious and have better relationship and commercial skills…
>
> Clive Chesser, CEO, Punch Pubs & Co

> In my experience, almost all the female ODs that have worked for me have been in the upper quartile of performance.
>
> Adam Fowle, ex-Senior NED, Ei Group

The relative outperformance of females compared to men at this level shouldn't come as a surprise to readers of this book, given that the top three outstanding OD competencies are behaviourally related – requiring excellent levels of *emotional/cultural intelligence*. But still there is an imbalance – why? According to both male and female respondents in this research study, under-representation of females at OD level can be explained by:

- o **Confidence** – the most cited impediment to female progression to OD was a lack of confidence, namely: due to socialisation (by society, parents, family, etc.), a lot of females suffered from a lack of self-esteem and self-worth, which held them back. In spite of being told by bosses that they were talented and capable of progression, females simply didn't believe the compliments! Women felt that they needed 80% of the skillset needed for the OD job before they put themselves forwards, whereas men applied with 50% (relying on front, bravery and bullshit to cover the rest off!). Potential solutions and interventions for OD developers?

- Coaching and mentoring of high-potential female AM/BDMs by strong role models.
- Scaffolding OD roles with safety nets, where females could build up confidence to do the fully fledged job.

o **Misogyny** – there was also a feeling amongst respondents that, particularly in the pub sector, women had been consciously or unconsciously discriminated against by senior male recruiters, who tended to pick ODs, MDs and CEOs in the image of themselves (gregarious, bombastic, 'driven' types, able to crack a joke). Although changing, there was a lingering perception that certain segments of the industry remained an old boys' club and that the erstwhile ALMR (Association of Licensed Multiple Retailers) had essentially been a 'festival of blokes'! Balancing mechanisms here?

- More females being promoted to MD and CEO level making recruitment decisions.
- Societal, generational and attitudinal change (over 75% of graduates coming into hospitality are females).

o **Family Break** – additionally – and quite obviously – females were perceived to be at a disadvantage to men if they chose to start a family at the 'prime promotional stage' of their career, in their 30s. Being away from the business on maternity leave meant losing momentum and 'disappearing from view', giving up ground to less-talented male candidates who were 'just there' when the vacancies come up. Transitioning back into work after perhaps a twelve-month break also presented problems in 'readjusting' and 'getting back up to speed'. Solutions here?

- More agile 'back-to-work' transitioning policies, procedures and systems.
- More considerate, equitable and responsive talent-management systems.

- o **Work–Life Balance** – also, the prospect of shooting for a highly pressurised OD job was highly off-putting to women with children who were concerned about the impact it could have on their work–life balance. With inequitable divisions of labour in many households, women were frightened at the prospect of being pulled away from home, covering large geographies with evening and weekend work, plus overnight stays. Solutions here?
  - Flexible working policies enabling female ODs to create their own work schedules and frameworks to fit both home and business requirements.
  - Greater working from home (using digital technology for meetings etc. to cut travel time).

In the war for talent, it is patently ludicrous that females – given their propensity to outperform men (as Simon Longbottom, Clive Chesser and Adam Fowle have acknowledged above) – are under-represented in the senior echelons of this industry. Although this is changing through more enlightened HR policies and approaches, more senior female operators at the apex of the industry (such as Karen Forrester, Helen Charlesworth, Susan Chappell, Elaine Kennedy, Liz Phillips and Vanessa Hall, in this book) are required to inspire and motivate the large cadre of women currently progressing through the middle ranks!

- **Do graduate ODs outperform non-graduate ODs?** – another question I asked the interviewees for this book was whether or not there was any performance differential between graduate and non-graduate ODs. Why? Confirmation, either way, would be of assistance to OD recruiters and developers, helping them to refine their selection criteria. Not surprisingly, there were a range of insights on the matter (reflecting the respondents' own personal experiences):
  - o **Graduates outperform non-graduates** – according to some of the respondents, graduates who 'stuck it out' and adapted to the 24/7 intensity of the hospitality industry eventually outperformed non-graduates. Why? Graduates have:
    - Better-developed analytical and critical-thinking skills (useful at a more strategic level)
    - Greater 'bandwidth', curiosity and capacity to learn (particularly handy in smaller companies where ODs will have field and functional responsibilities).

- o **Non-graduates outperform graduates** – however, for others – having witnessed the febrile behaviour of 'work-shy' graduates – non-graduates who have done the hard yards and risen through the ranks were deemed to be more effective at OD level. Why? Non-graduates have:
  - Greater credibility with the line, having 'been there, done it and got the tee-shirt!'
  - Superior people skills honed at successive levels within an industry where 'qualities trump qualifications'
  - Nous and guile and a better gut instinct (especially in L&T) to 'sense and neutralise danger' due to battle-scarred experiences
  - More incentive to prove people wrong and overa-chieve in a meritocratic sector that affords ambitious people second chances.

- o **ODs who have completed executive education courses outperform everyone** – generally, however, nearly all respondents agreed that the best predictor of performance was not whether ODs had or hadn't completed a university undergraduate degree; rather, it was whether or not they had done some formal executive education later on in their career! Why?
  - 'When the student is ready, the teacher will appear!'
  - The combination of experience and practice-based executive development strengthened their levels of self-awareness, insight and critical thinking
  - Executive education (as noted in the section 'Accel-erating OD Development', above) improves operator confidence, business vocabulary, writing skills and insight into crucial organisational interdependencies.

Clearly, outstanding ODs – as the prior research in this book has outlined – require sophisticated cultural, behavioural and cognitive-thinking skills. Experience bolsters the former; higher education augments the latter. OD recruiters and developers would do well to pay heed to candidates who have both.

In my view, it's not whether grads outstrip non-grads. Certainly, postgrads outstrip non-postgrads! Layering the exec postgrad development onto my operational experience increased my confidence and self-awareness. Once I had achieved that, I knew that I could achieve more.

Barry Robinson, National Operations Director, Parkdean Resorts

- **What types of ODs do businesses usually lack? (entrepreneurs, scalers, evolvers or turnaround specialists)** – dependent on business model type and their lifecycle position, different organisations require specific OD skills at particular times. According to respondents, three categorisations of businesses lacked certain ODs at various junctures:

    o **Start-Ups** – having nurtured entrepreneurial ODs in their early phases of development, as they get to scale, they generally lack ODs with 'systemising' skills:

Small companies lack systemiser ODs. Why? In-situ leaders are often too attached to running the business loosely through undocumented values and according to the founder's vision – although they usually have entrepreneurial and risk-taking mindsets in spades!

Gavin Smith, Managing Director, Pizza Pilgrims

    o **Managed Format Corporates** – by contrast, mature managed corporates often lacked entrepreneurs and risk-takers to drive transformational growth as they reached optimal scale:

All corporates lack OD trailblazers – game changers who have the courage to challenge the norms. You usually just get 'steady Eddies' in these environments…

Karen Forrester, ex-CEO, TGI Fridays

> Large multi-site managed leisure corporates tend to lack
> OD creative thinkers and entrepreneurs. They are usually
> so formulaic and like to keep things safe; tending to prefer
> 'tactical entrepreneurial' behaviours in limited ways, in limited
> amounts of sites…
>
> John Dyson, National Operations Director, Mecca Bingo

o **Leased and Tenanted** – in L&T environments where highly adaptive OD styles and expertise are required in a broad number of areas, ODs generally over-index in one area to the detriment of others:

> The truth is in L&T, you need a bit of everything. The problem
> is that you can become a jack of all trades, but master of none!
>
> Mike O'Connor, Operations Director, Greene King Pub Partners

So, what are the implications of these differing OD requirements for recruiters and developers? As tempting as it might be to foist big corporate 'systemisers' on small start-ups after their first signs of process breakdowns (due to scale), the consequences, in terms of values dilution and cultural misalignment, might prove costly. Also, transfusing big corporates with small-company OD entrepreneurial talent nearly always ends in disaster, when – after being strangled and frustrated by bureaucracy and slow decision-making – the 'bright new hopes' exit the business. The solution? Companies need to develop and stretch the competencies of the ODs they already have, or consciously expose themselves to the shock treatment of importing OD talent that might – at least over the short term – nudge them in the right direction.

# BRIEF SUMMARY

This chapter has complimented the previous one (addressing *what* the nine outstanding OD competencies are) by outlining *how* they are nurtured and developed, alongside a 'digressive discourse' on some frequently asked questions that might be of interest to OD developers. What are its findings?

- **Best Ways of Spotting OD Potential** – respondents ranked *high performance at AM level, Deputy OD/Senior AM impact* and *senior coaching/mentoring* as the best means of identifying OD potential. Further probing into these three areas established that aspirant ODs should focus upon ensuring that their potential is showcased by being a *leader amongst their peers, 'famous' for value-added acts and creating 'winning' cultures*, having a *high impact whilst deputising for their ODs* (rather than just holding the fort) and putting their hands up for *formal or informal coaching/mentoring* with senior executives (signalling their ambition).

- **Best OD Development Mechanisms** – once their *resilience* and *potential* has been spotted, the best means of developing outstanding ODs is to *transition them into 'strawberry-patch' OD roles*, expose them to *executive education* and *continue with senior coaching/mentoring* during their formative periods in the role. Why? Increasing their cognitive capacity and critical thinking through executive education and coaching/mentoring increases their bandwidth, giving them a more holistic perspective of strategic leadership and *organisational culture*, accelerating their *'Influencing and Alliance Building'* and *'Strategic Thinking'* competencies. Strawberry OD patch assignments improve *'Leading to Win'* and *'Building Capability'* competencies, facilitating *cultural experimentation* in safer, lower-risk environments.

- **Answers to Frequently Asked Questions:**

  o **Why do companies recruit external ODs?** – companies often opt for external rather than internal OD appointments due to unconscious bias, a need to avoid peer conflict, a lack of internal development mechanisms, risk reduction and change impact. Often these appointments fail due to a lack of *'cultural fit'* or an overestimation of the benefit they will add. *Interviewee Verdict: a mix of both external and internal appointments is healthy, but over-indexing with externals over internals can destabilise the business.*

  o **Do lifer AMs make better ODs than functional personnel?** – although lifers have deep tacit knowledge of field operations and service leadership, functional appointments can offer a fresh perspective, combined with fully honed influencing and alliance-building skills. *Interviewee Verdict: a* *combination of experience in the field and at the centre is pref-erable, but in the end, as long as the OD candidate is a great culture builder and is commercially strong, it doesn't matter!*

o **Why are there fewer female ODs?** – although most female ODs outperform their male counterparts (due to superior emotional/cultural intelligence, professionalism and atten-tion to detail), they are outnumbered at senior levels within the industry. Why? Four dominant reasons, namely: a lack of confidence, recruiter misogyny, family breaks and poor work–life balance. *Interviewee Verdict: more females can be transitioned into senior positions in the industry through supportive coaching/mentoring and 'scaffolding roles' that raise levels of confidence. Also, enlightened policies and proce-dures (flexible working, transparent recruitment processes, etc.) can be put in place by organisations to assist greater female progression.*

o **Are graduate ODs better than non-graduates?** – argu-ably, graduates that stick within the industry possess the agility, learning mindset and critical-thinking capabilities to go further than non-graduates. *Interviewee Verdict: 'qualities matter more than qualifications' in hospitality because of its high requirement for 'people centricity' skills and 24/7 reserves of stamina and resilience. Nevertheless, some form of further business education is useful for graduates or non-graduates prior to assuming the OD role.*

o **What skills do ODs lack?** – in smaller, start-up companies, ODs typically lack 'systemising' skills, whilst in large corporates they lack entrepreneurial and risk-taking skills. *Interviewee Verdict: think carefully before you try to overcompensate for skill gaps by recruiting big-company ODs into small companies or small-company ODs into large ones! Work with what you've got or recruit in the knowledge that after the initial 'big bang', the appointment probably won't last in the longer term.*

All of these insights should be of considerable assistance to aspirant ODs and their developers, preparing individuals for success at this level and alerting organisations to some of the pitfalls and challenges surrounding OD progression. But how do we bring all of the commentary and research we have presented and reviewed so far in this book into a more focused framework and checklist that summarises the *key* requirements and characteristics of this pivotal role? The concluding chapter, which follows, will attempt just such a task!

# CHAPTER FOUR
# CONCLUSION

In the Introduction, I outlined why the OD role is challenging due to the difficulties for ODs of closing down psychological and geographical *distance* with their units and teams, grappling with the *hospitality paradox* (extracting high energy, interactive service behaviours from a lowly paid, youthful and transient front-line workforce), getting to grips with the *financial complexity* and *scale of their portfolio*, and overcoming the *disruptive forces* of consumer behaviour changes and competitive pressures (particularly in light of the COVID pandemic). Delving further into the current context of the OD role in Chapter One, I highlighted the specific issues that the pandemic has thrown up for the hospitality sector, namely: *cashflow squeezes, category collapses, consumer changes, channel switches, ongoing cost pressures and a capability deficit (particularly in back-of-house and kitchen areas)*.

Nonetheless, I suggested that in spite of the enormous turbulence wrought by the pandemic, some positives emerged for organisations that managed 'to get to the other side', including: *leaner operations* and more *agile, collaborative and innovative cultures*. In turn, this increased responsiveness – induced by this apocalyptic event – would enable survivors to profit from future hospitality trends such as: a requirement for *safe socialisation*, increased *suburban/residential traffic* ('staying local'), a greater shift towards *smart technology* usage and *sustainable sourcing*, and *cravings for stimulating leisure experiences* and *shared social occasions*. At an individual level, although senior field operators within the industry experienced a high degree of *stress, loss* and *separation* during the pandemic, its sobering disruption increased their levels of *humility, perspective* and sense of *determination* to 'smash it' going into the new normal.

Interviewing twenty-seven senior executives (principally CEOs, MDs and ODs) spread across the sector, using a structured questionnaire (see Figure 1), I then sought to establish – in Chapter Two – the optimal shape of the OD role (its span of control and portfolio size) for various business model types. In addition, I located – through interviewees responses – the ideal 'stylistic centres of gravity' for ODs in these different business models, which turned out to be: *'streetfighter'* (unbranded managed), *'monomaniacal'* (single-branded managed), *'chameleon'* (multi-branded managed), *'negotiator'* (L&T) and *'policeman'* (franchised). Nonetheless, a consensus emerged that, whatever the dominant leadership style for each business model, a number of *competencies, qualities and key practices* could be ascribed to outstanding OD behaviour across the sector. What were they and how can they be more pertinently summarised for aspirant ODs and their developers?

# OUTSTANDING OD (OOD) MODEL AND FRAMEWORK

Throughout the book, I have included quotes from interviewees reflecting upon the characteristics and traits of poor ODs. Overwhelmingly, the interviewees alighted upon *leadership and behavioural deficiencies* as being their main blind spots – an insight that is reinforced by two further observations from respondents:

> Poor ODs are dictatorial and don't listen. They drive good people into the ground until they use up their mojo. Their focus is almost invariably 'short-term money' rather than 'long-term results' orientated…
>
> Doug Wright, CEO, Wright Restaurants T/A McDonald's Restaurants

> Poor ODs focus only upon their own needs. They are extremely susceptible to pressure from above and just transfer it downwards. To them, their people are pawns. They have personal ambition written all over their faces and always look after themselves rather than their people…
>
> John Dyson, National Operations Director, Mecca Bingo

Clearly, outstanding ODs do exactly the opposite. As the case studies have shown throughout the book, they passionately care about and energise their people, *creating open, inclusive, dynamic cultures* – a dominant predisposition that was surfaced and reinforced at every juncture during the research for this book. Thus, it is the singular ability above all others to *'programme the collective software' of their followers' minds* to **create vibrant, can-do, winning cultures** – without creating unquestioning cults (as Vanessa Hall highlighted in Case Study 9) – that separates the best from the rest, as the interviewees reiterated time and again during their accounts of outstanding practice:

*Create Trench Spirit*: really good ODs are great at imbuing elite tribes with what I call 'trench spirit': when the going gets tough, they've got teamers who will go over the top with them to capture back competitive territory!

Simon Longbottom, CEO, Stonegate Group

Also, the best ones – alongside constantly spotting sales opportunities – create a *calm '360-degree ring'* around them that exudes an *aura*. The team believes in them and aspires to be like them – a *trusted* leadership role model who presides over a *winning, can-do culture*.

Doug Wright, CEO, Wright Restaurants T/A McDonald's

Additionally, another contribution of this book is the insight – garnered from the structured interview research – that the most significant 'stretches' from the AM and OD role and the most important competencies of outstanding ODs are exactly the same, namely: *'Leading to Win'* and *'Building Capability'* (labelled 'Inspirational Leadership' by the respondents), coupled with *'Influencing and Alliance Building'* and *'Strategic Thinking'*. This is an important finding! Why? It suggests that the *cultural and leadership* competencies that make the execution of the role so important remain underdeveloped at a *managerially focused* AM level – the source of most OD talent. Whether this gap is also compounded by greater scale, distance or complexity, aspirant ODs and their developers must be left in no doubt that a failure to elevate *culturally and behaviourally related skills* will almost undoubtedly lead to severe delayed performance or outright failure.

Yet how can we concisely illuminate the skills, practices and qualities of outstanding ODs? Using the data and insights from the structured interviews and case-study narratives, I have been able to construct both an integrated OOD Model and associated OOD Framework, detailing the rank-ordered *competencies, qualities and key practices* of outstanding ODs, which should (I hope!) prove invaluable to prospective ODs and their coaches.

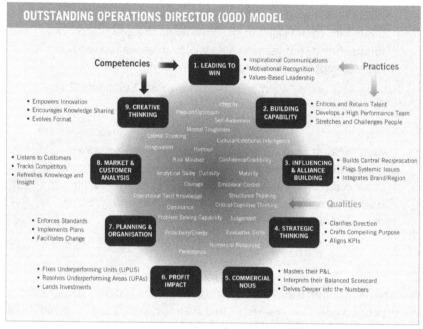

**Figure 3: Outstanding Operations Director (OOD) Model**

This model can be supplemented by a series of questions that ODs and potential ODs, or their developers, can use to assess levels of preparedness and/or capability:

## OOD Framework

### 1. LEADING TO WIN (self-awareness, mental toughness, credibility, confidence, integrity, cultural intelligence)

**Inspirational Communications**

'Do they inspire their AMs and regional tribe through uplifting face-to-face, written and digital communications (especially during adversity)?'

**Motivational Recognition**

'Do they spontaneously recognise and reward the contributions of their AMs and region/brand employees?'

**Values-Based Leadership**

'Do they agree a permitted code of conduct and consistently act with integrity, generating loyalty and trust amongst their AMs and wider regional/brand team?'

2. **BUILDING CAPABILITY (aspiration, emotional intelligence, judgement, listening skills)**

**Entices and Retains Talent**

'Do they fit the right people, with the right attitude, right energy and right skills into the right AM and regional/brand roles?'

**Develops a High-Performance Team**

'Do they care about the well-being, training, development, retention, succession and progression of their AM and regional/brand tribe?'

**Stretches and Challenges People**

'Do they provide challenging, honest coaching, mentoring and feedback which accelerates their AMs' performance capability?'

3. **INFLUENCING AND ALLIANCE BUILDING (social intelligence, maturity, diplomacy, emotional control)**

**Builds Central Reciprocation**

'Do they increase mutuality and reciprocity by helping key stakeholders (i.e. central and support functions) achieve their objectives?'

**Flags Systemic Problems**

'Do they courageously challenge central process and bureaucratic defects which seriously hamper field service delivery?'

**Integrates Region/Brand**

'Do they maturely navigate a path between regional/brand autonomy and central alignment?'

4. **STRATEGIC THINKING (critical and structured thinking, judgement and problem solving)**

**Clarifies Direction**

'Do they work with all relevant stakeholders to craft a clear, viable, growth-focused regional/brand budget and strategy?'

**Crafts Compelling Purpose**

'Do they co-design a noble purpose which creates real meaning and emotional resonance for their regional/brand tribe?'

**Aligns KPIs**

'Do they ensure regional/brand KPIs are aligned to strategic growth plans and are articulated/measured at ALL levels?'

### 5. COMMERCIAL NOUS (numerical reasoning, critical evaluation and cognitive thinking skills)

**Masters their P&L**

'Do they understand their region/brand's P&L numbers? Do they interpret patterns and join the dots within their portfolio?'

**Interprets their Balanced Scorecard**

'Do they process and understand the vital linkages, dependencies and connections within their region/brand's balanced scorecard?'

**Delves Deeper into the Regional/Brand Numbers**

'Do they dive further into the numbers (exception reports, etc.) and request customised financial information to inform impactful decisions?'

### 6. PROFIT IMPACT (courage, energy, operational tacit knowledge)

**Fixes UPUs (Underperforming Units)**

'Do they see the differences?'; 'Do they resolve the performance of UPUs that are a major "drag" upon their portfolio's numbers?'

**Resolves UPAs (Underperforming Areas)**

'Do they act decisively to turnaround failing districts (as benchmarked against the rest of the regional/brand portfolio)?'

**Lands Investments**

'Do they optimise site investments, consistently generating returns over and above internal capex ROI hurdles?'

### 7. PLANNING AND ORGANISATION (structured thinking, thoroughness, dominance, persistence)

**Enforces Standards**

'Do they act as the standard bearer for high-quality standards, safety, service, product, marketing, amenity and delivery in their region/brand?'

**Implements Plans**

'Do they prioritise, delegate and monitor impactful regional plans/actions that will meet/exceed company goals?'

**Facilitates Change**

'Do they urgently and effectively drive essential corporate change initiatives, on-time and on-budget?'

8. **MARKET AND CUSTOMER ANALYSIS (curiosity, analytical and processing skills)**

**Listens to Customers**

'Do they intimately know their sites and spend time on the ground observing trends and customer behaviour?'

**Tracks Competitors**

'Do they closely monitor competitive behaviour in their portfolio to identify threats and opportunities (to imitate or disrupt)?'

**Refreshes Knowledge and Insight**

'Do they constantly update their segment/sector knowledge through reading, networking and/or attending conferences?'

9. **CREATIVE THINKING (lateral thinking, imagination, risk-taking mindset)**

**Empowers Creativity**

'Do they empower their AMs and local teams to think and act creatively within a prescribed framework?'

**Encourages Knowledge Sharing**

'Do they encourage and facilitate knowledge and information swapping amongst their AMs and teams?'

**Evolves Format**

'Do they constantly seek to improve and extend the customer proposition in their formats (both digitally and land-based)?'

**Figure 4: Outstanding OD (OOD) Framework**

Both the OOD Model and the OOD Framework above should provide an elegant summary for those AMs who aspire to become an OD, existing ODs who wish strengthen their level of capability and developers of ODs who require an empirical checklist to inform their training programmes. Clearly – as stated – aspirant ODs and their developers need to primarily focus upon strengthening *cultural and behavioural leadership competencies*, accompanied by a 'push' on expanding *cognitive and critical-thinking faculties*. These can be accelerated – as Chapter Three outlined – through 'scaffolding OD positions' (strawberry patches or interim OD appointments), intensive senior coaching/ mentoring and executive education.

# PERSONAL QUALITIES

The OOD Model and OOD Framework above list a number of essential personal qualities that ODs require in order to master the nine essential competencies and twenty-seven practices underpinning outstanding OD performance. They are also mentioned at the top of each competency section within the book, but – up until now – I have been relatively silent regarding their efficacy and importance. Why? This book is intended for hospitality operators and developers who wish to master the 'art and science' of the OD role. It would have doubled in size if I'd given a blow-by-blow account of the individual personal qualities required for each competency and practice[17].

However, it suffices to say that the personal qualities I have alluded to in the sections, model and framework above will not come as a great surprise to the readers of this book! From a behavioural standpoint (for competencies such as Leading to Win, Building Capability, and Influencing and Alliance Building), outstanding ODs obviously need to be blessed with or develop a number of qualities, namely: *self-awareness, mental toughness, optimism, passion, integrity, emotional and cultural intelligence*, etc. From a technical and behavioural point of view (for competencies such as Strategic Thinking, Commercial Nous, Planning and Organisation, and Market and Customer Analysis) outstanding ODs need to develop and hone a number of personal qualities, namely: *critical thinking/reasoning, evaluative and problem-solving skills, analytical capabilities, operational tacit knowledge*, etc. Other qualities such as *dominance, energy (installed capacity to work) and courage* also reinforce the OD's credibility and impact within the field.

However, if I were to be pressed on which personal quality outstanding ODs require above all others, I would say – having developed scores of Area Managers that have ascended to the position (some of whom are showcased in this book) – that the most important requirement of all is *mental toughness*[18]. Supreme mental toughness – otherwise known as grit, resilience, resolve or hardiness – is the hallmark of outstanding ODs. The ability to keep calm, think

---

17  As stated throughout the book, Edger, C., and Heffernan, N., *Advanced Leader Coaching – Accelerating Personal, Interpersonal and Business Growth* (Oxford: Libri, 2020) and Edger, C., and Hughes, T., *Inspirational Leadership – Mobilising Super-performance through Emotion* (Oxford: Libri, 2017) both give comprehensive analyses and accounts of the personal qualities underpinning outstanding senior field leadership.

18  If you want to read beyond this book for further insights into polishing this *vital* quality, I highly recommend reading Angela Duckworth's *Grit – Why Passion and Resilience are the Secrets to Success* (New York: Vermillion, 2017).

clearly and retain a sense of equilibrium in highly charged situations, finding solutions to seemingly intractable problems, is what marks out the best from the rest. Senior field leadership in hospitality poses immense challenges, with so many complex moving parts. Indeed, the COVID pandemic over the past year has posed the ultimate resilience test to ODs – whatever business model they have presided over. Nonetheless, it is my observation that those that *keep their composure*, resonating determination and confidence in the face of (seemingly) insuperable odds, are the ones that ultimately prosper and succeed. But what are the characteristics of mentally tough leaders and how can this trait be strengthened and developed? The following article that I wrote for Propel sought to address these questions.

## *BEING AND BECOMING MENTALLY TOUGH*

**Chris Edger**

**(*Propel Quarterly*, Winter 2017)**

Over the last eight years, I have taught and coached over 700 Area Managers and Operations Directors – many of them from hospitality organisations – on our postgraduate Multi-Unit Leadership programmes at BCU. Over that time, we have measured their levels of mental toughness using the MTQ48 (Mental Toughness Questionnaire) psychometric test, highlighting specific areas that they can focus upon to improve their impact and effectiveness. Two things stand out from the tests. *First*, different genders have differing 'resilience' development needs; poor *emotional control stands out as the main issue for men*, whilst *lack of confidence is the Achilles heel for women. Second*, aggregate MTQ 48 scores[19] for all candidates have slipped over time. Why? Judging by feedback in our classroom and coaching sessions, the enormous stress and pressure of being in

---

19  The MTQ48 is a self-assessment psychometric built around four essential self-management components, namely: *control (emotional and life), challenge, commitment and confidence (abilities and interpersonal)*. By answering 48 questions relating to these components, respondents can measure their relative levels of mental toughness. Over the past decade on the postgraduate multi-unit programmes at BCU, all students (some 800 or so) have taken the MTQ48 online test as part of their 'Leading Service and Change' module. Empirical analysis of the questionnaire responses showed that the lowest stem score for *males* was *emotional control*, whilst *confidence in abilities* was the worst score for *females*. For further reading on the MTQ48 and its application, see Edger, C., and Heffernan, N., *Advanced Leader Coaching – Accelerating Personal, Interpersonal and Business Growth* (Oxford: Libri, 2020), pp. 35–47.

the 'squeezed middle' is intensifying rather than diminishing within organisations. However, over this period, we have had a number of students who have won ALMR Operations and Business Manager of the year awards and a fair proportion have progressed into senior executive positions within the industry. Isolating and delving into their MTQ48 scores and data, we discover that their psychometric scores were higher than the mean. They possessed more hardy characteristics! So, what stood out about them and how can mental toughness be developed?

In addition to obvious factors such having a *sense of perspective* (what is the worst thing that can happen?), *positive mind-set* and *surrounding themselves with likeminded people radiating energy*, three things characterise mentally tough managers and executives:

1. **Battle hardened** – the toughest steel is forged in the fiercest flame! Mentally tough managers have either consciously or inadvertently confronted and overcome adversity. They have been forced to operate outside their comfort zones, conquering tasks that had previously filled them with deep feelings of anxiety, apprehension and fear. This has given them *confidence*, making them far more courageous than their contemporaries. They have greater mental capacity to take on new challenges, coupled with an expectation and mind-set that they will succeed.

2. **Self-aware** – these winners also possess a degree of self-awareness that enables them to recognise and defuse negative thoughts and behavioural patterns. They are able to disrupt and *reframe negative 'internal conversations'* which threaten to immobilise and incapacitate them. This enables them to exercise far greater levels of emotional self-control than their peer group, meaning that they can concentrate on action and solutions rather than obsessing about setbacks, noise and distractions.

3. **Goal-focused** – the third thing that stands out about mentally tough operators is their *clear sense of purpose, aspiration and direction*. They know what they want and (broadly) how they are going to achieve it. That is to say, they are agile, flexible and open-minded enough to learn new skills and seek out essential resources to help them get there. Their goals are rarely improbable or delusional, being usually well thought out, realistic and

– compared to those of their contemporaries – slightly more stretching.

But is mental toughness a trait or a state? Is it genetic or can it be developed? Given the transformative impact that our development programmes have had on individuals that have suffered from cripplingly low scores in the MTQ48 test, I am firmly of the view that mental toughness is a state that can be nurtured and strengthened. How?

1. **Courageous coaching** – in my next book[20], I highlight how courageous coaching (using the BUILD–RAISE process) enables leader–coaches to help managers to build their levels of self-awareness, stiffen their resolve and move out of their comfort zone, principally by highlighting and *eliminating any 'interference'* that they believe to be inhibiting them. Very often, this interference is identified as lying *within* – a lack of courage, underpinned by misguided self-perceptions and perspectives – rather than *without*. Successful facilitation of the BUILD–RAISE coaching process helps fragile managers build their levels of insight, confidence, courage and – most crucially – impact.

2. **Reflective practice** – managers within hospitality run flat out, 24/7. They seldom have space to reflect and think about *what* they do, *why* they do it and *how* they could do it better. Also, because of ego, many operators are prone to apportioning blame to anybody but themselves for service breakdowns and failures. On our programmes, we see *managers grow as they critically reflect* upon their professional practice within their written work. *Making sense of themselves and their environment* provides a major boost to their overall effectiveness and well-being.

3. **Capacity-building skills** – in addition, those managers that have learnt the art and science of basic managerial skills (i.e. *strategic delegation, stakeholder influencing, action planning, time management, prioritisation, communication*, etc.) are far more likely to be more resilient. Why? Because they have built in capacity to innovate and focus upon achieving their superordinate goals.

---

20  For further reading on Courageous Coaching, see Edger, C., *Courageous Coaching using the BUILD–Raise Method* (Oxford: Libri, 2017). BUILD–RAISE is a pneumonic outlining a sequential coaching process, namely: Build Rapport, Understand Aim, Identify Interference, Locate Solutions and Determine Execution.

> Recently, Theresa May acknowledged that mental health issues were becoming a serious problem in UK society and spoke about how they needed to be addressed more openly and effectively. Businesses are not isolated from this phenomenon. Helping individuals to become more resilient and mentally tough is overlooked by most organisations, but paying heed to it can pay dividends in terms of productivity, creativity and energy. It is doubly important in the hospitality sector, where a long-hours culture, coupled with a notoriously poor reputation for safeguarding employee well-being, prevails. So, whilst learning the lessons from those who are mentally tough – *experiencing and conquering adversity, having high levels of self-awareness and clear goals* – we need to apply more of the developmental techniques that help managers increase their resilience and mental toughness. Organisations would benefit from training their leaders in courageous coaching techniques, encouraging more reflective practice and inculcating basic managerial skills so their people have more capacity to cope. Having a mentally tough cadre of managers is more important than ever in today's competitive environment; those organisations that choose to focus upon it will be surprised by its positive effect on the bottom line.

Let us be under no illusion: since I wrote that article, the intensification of the challenges confronting ODs has made the requirement for a mentally tough state of mind the role's primary prerequisite! The good news is – as the piece highlights – organisations can take positive action to strengthen the mental toughness of this pivotal cadre, through a number of development interventions.

But over and above the competencies, practices and qualities referenced so far in this book, what *skills* will ODs need to bolster over the next decade in order to be successful?

# FUTURE OD TRENDS

When interviewing the twenty-seven respondents, I was keen not just to make a rear-view-mirror analysis of outstanding OD skills and competency requirements. I also wanted to capture a forward-looking picture of the most important factors that would affect their practice, productivity and performance over the next decade. How? Using Korn Ferry's (2020) *six big technical leadership requirements* over the next decade, I asked the respondents *'What are the top two technical competencies that ODs will need to develop in order to outperform their peers over the next ten years?'* These were identified by the respondents as being (in rank order of importance):

1. **Customer Experience Design**
2. **Workplace Well-Being**
3. **Artificial Intelligence and Service Mechanisation**
4. **Digital Sales and Marketing**
5. **Big Data Analysis**
6. **Project Management.**

Thus, the future OD technical leadership requirements were rank-ordered, firstly, in terms of *customers* (customer experience design), secondly, in terms of *employees* (workplace well-being) and, thirdly, in terms of *technology, data analytics and project management.* This is to be expected: as the research findings in this book have highlighted, Leading to Win is the primary outstanding OD competency; outstanding ODs are principally concerned – as senior leaders of the field line – with galvanising and motivating their teams to delight their customers. Technology is an important component of this process, but it is an enabler and facilitator rather than memory generator! But what did the respondents have to say about the impact and importance of each macro-trend upon OD skills going forwards?

1. **Customer Experience Design** – given the timing of this research exercise, COVID featured front-of-mind for respondents, particularly in relation to the paramount importance that ODs would have to attach to getting the customer experience design right over the next decade:

   > Post-COVID, customers are going to become a lot more discerning – going out less, spending more – expecting more tailored experiences; ODs need to be at the forefront of this experiential re-design...
   >
   > Colin Hawkins, Divisional Operations Director,
   > Stonegate Group

> The challenge for premium-led ODs is – post-COVID (after sectioning tables off, dousing people in hand sanitiser, reducing 'customer touches' and speeding up the book–order–pay experience) – all about preventing a descent into depersonalisation...
>
> Martin Nelson, Operations Director, Premium Pub Group
> (Mitchells and Butlers)

2. **Employee Well-Being** – prior to COVID, addressing the industry skills shortage and winning the war for talent (particularly in the kitchens) would have been cited by respondents as one of the greatest HR-related challenges faced by ODs over the coming years. This undoubtedly remains a pressing issue. However, a mental-health epidemic – exacerbated by COVID – is now widely perceived by respondents as being one of the greatest challenges faced by ODs over the next decade:

> The mental health challenge has created a perfect storm for ODs in hospitality. How? First, the media has made disclosing mental-health problems fashionable, with celebrities setting the trend. It's no longer a taboo subject. Second, we have a disproportionate number of under-25s (millennials) in our workforce, who are more susceptible and vulnerable to well-being issues due to the challenges posed by social media. So, this isn't going to go away and COVID has compounded it. In the short to medium term, it will come down to businesses and ODs to do a lot of 'people fixing' over the coming years...
>
> Helen Charlesworth, Executive MD, Stonegate Pub Company

3. **Artificial Intelligence and Service Mechanisation** – with increasing costs pressing down upon the industry (exacerbated by annual living wage hikes and rising input costs), respondents placed the likelihood of AI adoption and service mechanisation – as potential cost mitigators – third in the order of priorities for ODs to master over the next decade:

And technology will replace some of the largest cost: human labour. COVID has been a real accelerator and wake-up call for in-premise food and drinks occasions (speeding up book–order–delivery–pay). Post-COVID, it will be deemed less important for customers to see chefs or someone at the table; what they will really crave are social occasions and celebrations combined with seamless service/delivery. Technology will be the enabler for this and ODs have to understand how they will adapt their operational models accordingly...

Karen Forrester, ex-CEO, TGI Fridays

4. **Digital Sales and Marketing** – prior to the pandemic, digital sales and marketing adoption in the hospitality was sporadic, with large corporates and fast-food firms leading the way. The COVID pandemic speeded up the adoption of digital book–order–pay systems throughout the sector out of necessity. Given that so much of their units' service cycles will now take place online and become digitally enhanced 'in premise', ODs will have to step up and take greater ownership of critical 'sensitivity points' within their new 'digital steps of service':

Up to now, for most experienced ODs, digital has seemed like a dark art practised by other functions. ODs just haven't developed a sufficient in-depth understanding or ownership of the digital customer cycle. But given how customers are being digitally educated by other industries and the leap forward our sector was required to make during COVID, we need (as ODs) to put more time and energy into it! We need to encourage and leverage strong interdependencies between all of our functions that are engineering the way in which we will digitally interact with our customers in the future to maximise throughputs and spend-per-head.

Colin Hawkins, Divisional Operations Director,
Stonegate Group

5. **Big Data Analysis** – a natural by-product of greater digital interaction with customers in hospitality will be the availability of a voluminous amount of data on customer preferences and behaviour. The challenge for ODs will be to disaggregate key insights from this statistical mountain to inform value-added decision-making. Having more data is great, but deciphering what really matters will be key:

> Tesco have been the leaders in customer analytics (though their Clubcard data) for a couple of decades. Hospitality has been way behind the curve on this. But it is coming, with greater digitalised interaction. The trick will lie in deciphering the high levels of data that pour through the 'box' and deciding which levers to pull! The best ODs will use big data to support or overturn their own gut instincts – but their operational interpretation of the data and what needs to be implemented to drive traffic and sales will still remain crucial...
>
> James Pavey, National Operations Director, Tesco Cafés

6. **Project Management** – COVID not only made many hospitality businesses take a giant digital leap forward, it also speeded up their capacity to successfully implement critical changes and initiatives in timeframes that would hitherto have been regarded as impossible. Of course, COVID and on the hoof government policy provided the burning platform for this heightened responsiveness. As the industry emerges into the post-pandemic new normal – with new strains, variants and scaremongering threatening further disruption – ODs will remain at the forefront of project managing new ways of working throughout their portfolios:

> As the industry emerges out of the COVID tornado, ODs will still need good project-management skills to implement complex changes. This isn't going to go away, in the short or medium term, until there is a comprehensive medical solution. Given the health-and-safety restrictions organisations will have to abide by, organisations will constantly need to keep thinking about how they can constantly adapt their pubs to make them work for customers *and* the P&L. This will involve a lot of quick planning and flawless implementation.
>
> Adam Fowle, ex-Senior NED, Ei Group

Clearly, as they reflected on the major trend areas for ODs over the next ten years, the interviewees (as illustrated by their comments) viewed the COVID pandemic and its inevitable aftershocks as playing a major role in shaping OD priorities going forwards. But what does this actually mean for ODs – what do they need to do to personally equip themselves for these new challenges? In reality, the answer to this question hardly deviates from the main findings and substance of this book. In the future, the main competencies, qualities and practices that ODs will require to be successful will remain the same as they were before – but with one subtle difference: ODs will need to *dial up* their critical behavioural, cognitive and technical faculties to reenergise and reinvigorate their businesses. Evolving the customer experience and improving employee well-being will require a further step up in *behavioural leadership capabilities*; not least because this will have to be achieved within the *context of enormous change*, with a switch to smarter digital and AI technologies to drive sales and contain costs. The way they navigate and land these changes will not only require deft people skills, but significant *cognitive thinking and project-management capability*. Thus, as the intensity of change within the industry ramps up, ODs will have no choice other than to master the competencies and practices outlined in this book – or be prepared to fail faster and bigger than before!

# FINAL WORDS

In this book – the first of its kind – I wanted to define more precisely the role, competencies and practices of the senior field leader, namely: the Operations Director. The role is a source of fascination to me, not only because of its strategic importance to hospitality organisations, but because so many of my students over the years on my Multi-Unit Leadership and Strategy programmes have asked me *how* they can get promoted into the role and *what* they have to do to be successful when they get there! Indeed, many of them have written assignments and dissertations relating to various dimensions of the role. Additionally, having been an Operations Director myself (albeit over twenty-five years ago), I passionately wished to explore and understand the main drivers that underpin its success at this current time.

There is little doubt that the COVID pandemic has wreaked havoc upon the hospitality industry during the writing of this book. As I have argued, it will impact consumer and industry behaviour for some time to come. Nevertheless, the in-premise drinking/dining out sector will rise again! Arguably, the effects of lockdowns and severe restrictions have highlighted – more than ever – *the visceral human craving for a convivial hospitality sector where people can commune together, enjoying shared, uplifting experiences.* To this extent, as we advance into the post-COVID 'new normal', hospitality organisations will still require outstanding Operations Directors to *lead, inspire and drive change* throughout their hospitality field operations. Thus, far from being surplus to requirements, the outstanding OD will be in great demand as the industry regenerates itself during the so-called 'roaring twenties'.

So – boiling everything in this book right down – what do outstanding hospitality ODs do? Occupying a pivotal position between the centre and the field, the best ones are *synthesisers, intermediaries, articulators, aligners, translators, advocates, advisors, coaches, interpreters, scanners, resource-hunters, negotiators, trouble-shooters, delegators, enforcers and implementers.* But above all, they are this: intuitively understanding that *culture* is the assassin of their biggest enemy – geographical/psychological *distance* from their people – *outstanding ODs are mentally tough, inspiring leaders who **ignite distinctive regional/brand cultures**, mobilising their tribes to achieve exceptional performance and growth!* That is the main takeout that *all* aspirant ODs and their developers should extract from this book.

# SOURCES AND FURTHER READING

Aaron Allen & Associates (2016) The Cost of Pissed Off Employees Quantified. https://aaronallen.com/blog/associate-engagement-cost-of-pissed-off-employees-quantified.

Ansoff, I. (1968) *Corporate Strategy*. London: Penguin Publishing.

Bass, B.M. (1985) *Leadership and Performance Beyond Expectation*. New York: Free Press.

Bass, B.M., and Bass, R. (2008) *The Bass Handbook of Leadership: Theory, Research, and Managerial Applications* (4th ed.). NY: Free Press.

Belbin, R.M. (2000a) *Team Roles at Work*. NY: Butterworth-Heinemann.

Belbin, R.M. (2000b) *Beyond the Team*. NY: Butterworth-Heinemann.

Berry, L. (2000) Cultivating Service Brand Equity. *Academy of Marketing Science*, 28(1): 128–37.

Blanchard, K. (2007) *Leading at a Higher Level*. London: Prentice Hall.

Blanchard, K., Carew, D., and Parisi Carew, E. (2004) *The One Minute Manager Builds High Performing Teams*. London: Harper Collins.

Blanchard, K., and Johnson, S. (1986) *The One Minute Manager*. New York: Harper Collins.

Burns, T., and Stalker, G.M. (1961) *The Management of Innovation*. London: Tavistock.

Byford, M., Watkins, M., and Triantogiannis, L. (2017) *Onboarding isn't Enough. Harvard Business Review*, 1 May.

Chandler, A.D. (1962) *Strategy and Structure*. Boston MA: MIT Press.

Christensen, C.M., and Overdorf, M. (2000) Meeting the Challenge of Disruptive Change. *Harvard Business Review*, 78(2), March–April: 67–76.

Clough, P., and Strycharczyk, D. (2015) *Developing Mental Toughness: Coaching Strategies to Improve Performance, Resilience and Wellbeing* (2nd ed.). London: Kogan Page.

Clutterbuck, D. (2014) *Everyone Needs a Mentor*. London: CIPD.

Clutterbuck, D., and Megginson, D. (2015) *Making Coaching Work – Creating a Coaching Culture*. London: CIPD.

Cohen, A.R., and Bradford, D.L. (1989) *Influence without Authority*. NY: John Wiley.

Collins, J. (2001) *Good to Great: Why Some Companies Make the Leap… and Others Don't*. London: Random House.

Collins, J., and Porras, J. (1994) *Built to Last: Successful Habits of Visionary Companies*. London: Random House.

Covey, S.R. (1989) *The 7 Habits of Highly Effective People*. London: Simon & Schuster.

De Bono, E. (1985) *Six Thinking Hats: An Essential Approach to Business Management*. Boston: Little Brown and Company.

de Chernatony, L. (2001) A Model for Strategically Building Brands. *Brand Management*, 9(1): 32–44.

de Chernatony, L., and McDonald, M. (1992) *Creating Powerful Brands*. London: Butterworth Heinemann.

de Chernatony, L., and Segal-Horn, S. (2003) The Criteria for Successful Services Brands. *European Journal of Marketing*, 37(7/8): 1,095–118.

de Vries, M.F., Korotov, K.R., and Florent-Treacy, E. (2007) *Coach or Couch: The Psychology of Making Better Leaders*. Paris: INSEAD Business Press.

Deci, E. (1972) Intrinsic Motivation, Extrinsic Reinforcement and Inequity. *Journal of Personality and Social Psychology*, 22(1): 113–20.

Dobelli, R. (2013) *The Art of Thinking Clearly*. London: Sceptre.

Doltlich, D. (2006) *Leadership Passages: The Personal and Professional Transitions That Make or Break a Leader*. London: CIPD.

Doran, G. (1981) There's a S.M.A.R.T. Way to Write Management's Goals and Objectives. *Management Review*, 70(11): 35–6.

Downey, M. (2003) *Effective Coaching: Lessons from the Coach's Coach*. London: Texere Publishing.

Drucker, P.F. (1989) *The Practice of Management* (9th ed.). London: Heinemann Professional.

Duckworth, A. (2017) *Grit – Why Passion and Resilience are the Secrets to Success*. New York: Vermillion.

Dweck, C. (2017) *Mindset: Changing the Way You Think to Fulfil Your Potential*. New York: Ballantine Books.

Edger, C. (2012) *Effective Multi-Unit Leadership – Local Leadership in Multi-Site Situations*. Farnham: Gower Business Publishing.

Edger, C. (2013) *International Multi-Unit Leadership – Developing Local Leaders in Multi-Site Operations*. Farnham: Gower Business Publishing.

Edger, C. (2014) *Professional Area Management – Leading at a Distance in Multi-Unit Enterprises* (1st ed.). Oxford: Libri.

Edger, C. (2015) *Professional Area Management – Leading at a Distance in Multi-Unit Enterprises* (2nd rev. ed.). Oxford: Libri.

Edger, C. (2016) *Area Management – Strategic and Local Models for Growth*. Oxford: Libri.

Edger, C. (2018) *Courageous Coaching – Using the BUILD–RAISE Model* (A Practical Guide for Leader–Coaches). Oxford: Libri.

Edger, C. (2019) *Coaching Star Performers – Reframing Negative Drivers and Feelings*. Oxford: Libri.

Edger, C., and Emmerson, A. (2015) *Franchising – How Both Sides Can Win*. Oxford: Libri.

Edger, C., and Heffernan, N. (2020) *Advanced Leader Coaching – Accelerating Personal, Interpersonal and Business Growth*. Oxford: Libri.

Edger, C., and Hughes, T. (2016) *Effective Brand Leadership – Be Different. Stay Different. Or Perish*. Oxford: Libri.

Edger, C., and Hughes, T. (2017) *Inspirational Leadership – Mobilising Super-performance Through eMOTION*. Oxford: Libri.

Edger, C., and Oddy, R.E. (2018) *Events Management – 87 Models for Event, Venue and Experience Managers*. Oxford: Libri.

Edger, C., and Tucker, M. (2019) *Coaching Senior Hires – Transitioning Potential into Performance Quickly!* Oxford: Libri.

Egon Zehnder (2017) in 'Onboarding Isn't Enough'. *Harvard Business Review*. May–June 2017.

Elsner, R., and Farrands, B. (2012) *Leadership Transitions: How Business Leaders Take Charge in New Roles*. London: Kogan Page.

French, J., and Raven, B. (1959) 'The Bases of Social Power', in D. Cartwright, *Studies in Social Power*. Ann Arbor, MI: Institute for Social Research, pp. 150–67.

George, B., Sims, P., McLean, A.N., and Meyer, D. (2007) Discovering Your Authentic Leadership. *Harvard Business Review*, February: 129–38.

Gladwell, M. (2008) *Outliers: The Story of Success*. NY: Little, Brown and Co.

Goffee, R., and Jones, G. (2006) *Why Should Anyone Be Led by You? What It Takes to Be an Authentic Leader*. Boston MA: Harvard Business School Press.

Goleman, D. (1996) *Emotional Intelligence*. NY: Bloomsbury.

Goleman, D. (1998) *Working with Emotional Intelligence*. NY: Bantam Books.

Haeckel, S.H., and Nolan, R.L. (1993) Managing by Wire. *Harvard Business Review*, 71, September–October: 122–32.

Hamel, G. (2000) Waking Up IBM: How a gang of Unlikely Rebels Transformed Big Blue. *Harvard Business Review*, July–August: 137–44.

Hamel, G., and Prahalad, C. (1990) *The Core Competence of the Corporation*. London: Macat.

Hase, S., Davies, A., and Dick, B. (1999) *The Johari Window and the Dark Side of Organisations*. SCU: USA.

Hersey, P., and Blanchard, K.H. (1969) Life cycle theory of leadership. *Training and Development Journal*, 23: 26–35.

Hersey, P., and Blanchard, K.H. (1993) *Management of Organizational Behavior: Utilizing Human Resources* (6th ed.). NY: Prentice-Hall.

Herzberg, F. (1959) *The Motivation to Work*. New York: Wiley.

Herzberg, F. (1987) One More Time: How Do You Motivate Employees? *Harvard Business Review*, September–October.

Heskett, J., Jones, T., Loveman, G., Sasser, W., and Schelsinger, L. (1994) Putting the Service Profit Chain to Work. *Harvard Business Review*, March–April: 164–74.

Heskett, J.L., Sasser, W.E., and Schlesinger, L.A. (2003) *The Value Profit Chain*. NY: The Free Press.

Hofstede, G., Hofstede, G.J., and Minkov, M. 2010. *Cultures and Organisations* (3rd ed.). New York: McGraw-Hill.

House, R.J. (1971) A Path-Goal Theory of Leadership Effectiveness. *Administrative Science Quarterly*, 16: 321–38.

Janis, I. (1972) *Victims of Groupthink*. Boston: Houghton Mifflin.

Johnston, R. (2001) *Service Excellence = Reputation = Profit.* Institute of Customer Service.

Kahneman, D. (2012) *Thinking, Fast and Slow.* London: Penguin.

Kellerman, B. (2008) *Followership: How Followers are Creating Change and Changing Leaders.* London: Penguin.

Kobasa, S.C. (1979) Stressful life events, personality and health: An enquiry into hardiness. *Journal of Personality and Social Psychology*, 37: 1–11.

Korn Ferry International (2020) *Accelerating through the Turn – Shaping the Future Workforce.* Global Survey Paper, 20 April.

Kotter, J.P. (1982) What Effective General Managers Really Do. *Harvard Business Review*, 60(6): 156–62.

Kotter, J.P. (1996) *Leading Change.* Boston: Harvard Business Press.

Kübler-Ross, E. (1997) *On Death and Dying.* New York: Simon & Shuster.

Levitin, D. (2014) *The Organized Mind.* London: Penguin.

Levitt, T. (1980) Marketing Success through Differentiation – of Anything. *Harvard Business Review*, January–February.

Lewin, K. (1951) *Field Theory in Social Science.* New York: Harper and Row.

Lindblom, C. (1959) The Science of Muddling Through. *Public Administration Review*, 19: 79–88.

Locke, E. (1968) Toward a Theory of Task Motivation and Incentives. *Organisational Behaviour and Human Performance*, 3: 157–89.

McKinsey (2006) The 'Moment of Truth' in Customer Service. *McKinsey Quarterly.* February.

McKinsey (2008) Maintaining the Customer Experience. *McKinsey Quarterly.* December.

Mann, C. (2016) *The 6th Ridler Report – Strategic Trends in Coaching.* London: Ridler.

Martin, J. (2014) For Senior Leaders, Fit Matters More Than Skill. *Harvard Business Review*, January 17.

Maslow, A. (1943) *Motivation and Personality.* Republished 1987 edition – Hong Kong: Longman Asia Ltd.

Mintzberg, H. (1973) *The Nature of Managerial Work.* NY: Harper Row.

Mintzberg, H. (1979) *The Structuring of Organisations*. NY: Prentice Hall.

Mintzberg, H. (1987) Crafting Strategy. *Harvard Business Review*, 65: 66–75.

Mintzberg, H. (2009) *Managing*. London: Pearson.

Mintzberg, H., Ahlstrand, B., and Lampel, J. (1998) *Strategy Safari*. NY: Free Press.

Morris, J., Brotheridge, C., and Urbanski, J. (2005) Bringing Humility to Leadership: Antecedents and Consequences of Leader Humility. *Human Relations*, 58: 1,323–49.

Naude, J., and Plessier, F. (2014) *Becoming a Leader-Coach: A Step-by-Step Guide to Developing Your People*. CCL: USA.

Nayar, V. (2010) *Employees First, Customers Second*. Boston: Harvard Business School Press.

Nonaka, I., and Takeuchi, H. (1995) *The Knowledge Creating Company*. New York: Oxford University Press.

Nonaka, I., and Takeuchi, H. (2011) The Wise Leader. *Harvard Business Review*, May: 58–67.

O'Reilly, C., and Tushman, M. (2004) The Ambidextrous Organisation. *Harvard Business Review*, April: 74–81.

Passmore, J. (2015) *Leadership Coaching: Working with Leaders to Develop Elite Performance*. London: Kogan Page.

Peters, S. (2012) *The Chimp Paradox: The Mind Management Programme to Help You Achieve Success, Confidence and Happiness*. London: Vermilion.

Pfeffer, J. (1994) *Competitive Advantage through People*. Boston MA: Harvard Business School Press.

Pfeffer, J. (1998) *The Human Equation: Building Profits by Putting People First*. Boston MA: Harvard Business School Press.

Pink, D. (2009) *Drive – The Surprising Truth About What Motivates Us*. London: Canongate Books.

Porter, M. (1985) *Competitive Advantage: Creating and Sustaining Superior Performance*. NY: Free Press.

Porter, M.E. (1987) Corporate Strategy: The State of Strategic Thinking. *Economist*, May 23: 17–22.

Raven, B.H., and French, J.R.P. (1958) Legitimate power, coercive power, and observability in social influence. *Sociometry*, 21: 83–97.

Reichheld, F. (2003) One Number You Need to Grow. *Harvard Business Review*. December.

Riddle, D. (2017) Equipping Transitioning Leaders for Success. *Center for Creative Leadership Report*.

Rock, D. (2008) SCARF: A Brain-based Model for Collaborating with and Influencing Others. *NeuroLeadership Journal*: 1–21.

Schein, E. (1985) *Organizational Culture and Leadership: A Dynamic Review*. San Francisco: Josey-Bass.

Schein, E. (2013) *Humble Enquiry – The Gentle Art of Asking Instead of Telling*. CA: Berrett-Koehler.

Seligman, M. (2011) *Flourish*. Australia: William Heinemann.

Selznick, P. (1957) *Leadership in Administration. A Sociological Interpretation*. Evanston IL: Peterson.

Senge, P. (2005) *The Fifth Discipline: The Art and Practice of the Learning Organisation*. London: Random House.

Sinek, S. (2011) *Start with Why: How Leaders Inspire Everyone to Take Action*. London: Penguin.

Sinek, S. (2017) *Leaders Eat Last: Why Some Teams Pull Together and Others Don't*. London: Penguin.

Sinek, S. (2019) *The Infinite Game: How Businesses Achieve Long-Lasting Success*. London: Penguin.

Skinner, B.F. (1965) *Science and Human Behaviour*. NY: Free Press.

Skinner, B.F. (1976) *About Behaviorism*. NY: Vintage Bodis.

Starr, J. (2016) *The Coaching Manual: The Definitive Guide to the Process, Principles and Skills of Personal Coaching* (4th ed.). Harlow: Pearson.

Syed, M. (2016) *Black Box Thinking: Marginal Gains and the Secrets of High Performance*. London: John Murray.

Terman, L.M. (1904) A Preliminary Study in the Psychology and Pedagogy of Leadership. *Pedagogical Seminary*, 11(4): 413–83.

Tuckman, B., and Jensen, M.A. (1977) Stages of Small-Group Development Revisited. *Group & Organisation Studies*, 2(4): 419–27.

Turner, P., and Kalman, D. (2014) *Make Your People Before You Make Your Products*. London: John Wiley & Sons.

Vroom, V.H., and Yetton, P.W. (1973) *Leadership and Decision-Making.* Pittsburgh: University of Pittsburgh Press.

Walker, M. (2017) *Why We Sleep.* London: Penguin.

Whitmore, J. (2009) *Coaching for Performance: The Principles and Practices of Coaching and Leadership.* London: Nicholas Brealey.

Wilkinson, M. (2013) *The Ten Principles Behind Great Customer Experiences.* Harlow: FT Publishing.

Young, P. (2004) *Understanding NLP: Principles and Practice* (2nd ed.). Carmarthen: Crown.

Zaleznik, A. (1977) Managers and Leaders: Are They Different? *Harvard Business Review*, May–June: 67–78.